ACKNOWLEDGEMENTS:

COVER ART

The painting on the cover of this book was done
by my cousin, Edward Gifford. He was a well
known local artist and much of his work focused
on Amish themes. He always included a red bird
in his paintings. When my first dog, Timmie,
died, he sent me this drawing as an expression
of his sympathy.

ILLUSTRATIONS

The line drawings which appear throughout this
book were done by the 5th and 6th Grade students
at St. Vincent Elementary School in Akron, Ohio. I
gave the students a few of the stories that appear in
the book and asked them to choose a line from the
story to illustrate. Most of the students participated
and it was difficult to choose the drawings to use for
the book. I wish I could have used all of them, but
that was not possible. I want to thank all the
students who submitted drawings.

OTHERS

Thanks to John Pressello for preparing the graphics;
to Steve Halaiko and Robert (Sharkey) Johnson for
proofreading the text.

INTRODUCTION

My first book, *Vinnie Here*, was a collection of stories based on a variety of topics, none of which had any necessary connection to another. Such an arrangement left me free to choose my favorite stories from the many I had written over the years for our parish bulletin. Hoping to increase the usefulness of these stories, most of which grew out of my various experiences with Vinnie, I included an introduction to each and suggestions for further discussion or reflection.

I was pleasantly surprised to learn that my readers found *Vinnie Here* an enjoyable book to read. That alone would have been enough to satisfy my doubting the value of my efforts. Even more satisfying was learning the ways in which *Vinnie Here* was being used.

One writer, whom I met at the desk of Vinnie's hospital, told me she was using it for her RCIA scripture sharing. Another, a guidance counselor in a public school, wrote to tell me she was using it to teach values to children in primary grades. She was good enough to send me the letters her children had written to Vinnie. I was deeply touched by the hurt lying beneath their words and the way Vinnie was able to bring them comfort. I am constantly amazed at the healing powers a dog has for both the young and the old.

Responses such as these convinced me of the value of continuing my Vinnie stories along the lines of the title I had originally intended for my book. Using the themes of the gospels for the Sundays and liturgical celebrations of the year, I have written a story for each week of the year. It is my fervent hope that these whimsical reflections on the gospels will be helpful for personal prayer as well as for group sharing of every kind.

Thank you, kind reader, for your encouragement and support. May you enjoy the year with Vinnie as much as I have enjoyed living it with him.

ADVENT SEASON

FIRST SUNDAY OF ADVENT
Matthew 24:37-44

Advent is a time of waiting for the coming of the Lord. For children it is a time of waiting for Christmas and receiving gifts. For parents it is a busy time of buying gifts and throwing or attending parties. Celebrations and gift-giving are the means we use for remembering the birth of Jesus. But Advent is more than that. It is a time to prepare for the coming of the Lord into our lives each day and at the end of our lives some day. The best way to prepare for the ongoing coming of Christ is to keep the Lord always in our minds through prayer (watchful waiting) and through acts of virtue and generosity, bringing the presence of Jesus to others and being ready to greet him when he comes again.

WATCHING AND WAITING

You went outside pretty early this morning, Vinnie. What is it you were so interested in at that hour of the day?

I was just sitting by the gate, waiting to see who showed up.

Is there anybody in particular you were looking for?

As a matter of fact, boss, yes there was. There are several people I watch for each morning.

What's so special about those people, Vinnie?

If you really have to know, boss, we have a kind of agreement between us.

You do? What kind of agreement?

Basically, I agree to sit out here and wait for them, and they agree to bring me some treats. It all works out quite well, and I think the exchange is eminently equitable.

I don't know about that, Vinnie. It seems to me that you're getting more than you are giving.

I suppose it might appear that way on the surface, boss, but you have to examine it a little more closely.

And what will that tell me, Vinnie?

You see, boss, you'll find that my being here and faithfully waiting brings a great deal of pleasure to these folks. I get their day off to a good start. I think it has to do with that "more pleasure in giving than in receiving" thing you always talk about.

You've got a point there, Vinnie, but let me ask you a question. What happens on those days when these friends of yours don't come to church? It seems you're out here waiting regardless.

I've never thought about it, boss, but you're right. You see, one never knows when the person with treats might come. Sometimes it's a person I've never met before, who just happens to show up with treats. If I weren't waiting at times like that, I might miss something. One can never give up waiting, knowing that the day will come when the waiting will be rewarded with something really good.

I've got to hand it to you, Vinnie. You surprise me with your understanding of things. Now I know why you wait each morning at the kitchen door for Karen to show up. She always brings you something. But I'm afraid Karen isn't coming today, Vinnie. It's her day off.

Will you never learn, boss? Now please open the back door. Karen may just show up, and if so, I'll be waiting.

Reflection:
1. Am I already satisfied and no longer interested in waiting for the coming of Jesus?
2. What would I want Jesus to bring me this Christmas?
3. How can I put into practice this mode of waiting?

SECOND SUNDAY OF ADVENT

Matthew 3:1-12

COURSE CORRECTION

Each year, as we prepare for the celebration of Christmas, we listen to the preaching of John the Baptist, who came to prepare a way for the Lord. Preparing ourselves for the coming of Christ into our lives means making room for him in our hearts by eliminating the selfishness which leads us to sin. The glamour of the Christmas season and the intensity of the advertisements which seek to draw us away from God and toward the things of this world are directly opposed to the message of Christmas that Christ is the center of our lives and all that is necessary for us to find happiness. John the Baptist reminds us to turn away from all that distracts us from finding Jesus.

What are you barking about, Vinnie? It's enough to wake the dead.

What do you think I'm barking about, boss? Can't you see I'm standing out here on the deck all by myself? For heaven's sake, let me in!

If you're so anxious to come in, why did you go out in the first place?

It wasn't my decision, boss. I was duped into going out.

How did that happen?

It was Sister. She got me to follow her by tempting me with a biscuit, and before I knew it, she was inside and I was outside.

Now why would Sister do something like that, Vinnie?

That's what I was wondering, boss. I was in the kitchen, as usual, helping her clean up after supper, and the next thing I know, I'm standing out here on the deck.

Hold on a second, Vinnie. Did you say you were helping her clean up?

That's right, boss. Just like always.

Did Sister ask for your help, Vinnie, or did you just presume that she needed it?

You know how it is, boss. She always says things like: "Now Vinnie, behave yourself," or "Now Vinnie, you know you shouldn't do that." But she doesn't mean it.

Why would she say such things, Vinnie? You don't do anything wrong, do you?

I don't think so, boss. Sister has a habit of putting leftover dishes on the counter or on the table, so I just give her an assist by emptying them before she puts them in the dishwasher.

Has it ever occurred to you, that maybe she didn't want those dishes emptied? It may well be that she intended to save them for another meal.

The thought crossed my mind, boss, but I never took it too seriously. The temptation just gets the best of me.

I think I'm beginning to understand why you were outside just now—you were unceremoniously put out.

I think I knew that boss. I just didn't want to confess it to you.

Maybe it's time you considered changing your ways, Vinnie. Christmas is coming, and it's a good time to make some course corrections.

Sounds good, boss. Which course should I begin with?

Reflection:
1. What distracts me from following Christ completely?
2. Is Christmas the spiritual feast it should be?
3. How can I make Christmas a more spiritual event?

It's enough to wake the dead.

TYLER GILCHRIST

THIRD SUNDAY OF ADVENT

Isaiah 35: 1-6a, 10

Isaiah's dream of the peaceable kingdom where natural enmities will cease and suffering will be no more are part of our prayer, as we prepare for the coming celebration of Christmas. We believe that Jesus came to bring to fulfillment that wonderful vision of the prophet who waits for the day of redemption. Events in our world remind us that the dream is not yet realized. For the dream to come true, each one of us must make the dream our own and do whatever we can to wipe out the causes of war and suffering. The good works we do at Christmas are only the beginning of a task it will take a lifetime to complete.

SCAT CAT

Take it easy, Vinnie, you're nearly pulling me over.

Well come on, boss, get a move on.

What's the matter with you, Vinnie? Why are you barking so?

It's that cat.

Do you mean the cat looking out the window at us?

That's the one, boss. Look at him sitting there so smug. Who does he think he is?

But, Vinnie, the cat lives in that house. He has a right to sit in the window and see what's going on outside. He isn't bothering you, so why are you getting so upset?

I can't help it, boss. It's just that cats really bother me. Don't ask me why, I just have to go after any cat I see. I guess I was born that way.

That doesn't make a whole lot of sense, does it Vinnie? I mean why should you pick a fight with that cat? He never did anything to you, except get you all upset by looking out the window.

You're right, boss. I shouldn't be so angry just because there's a cat looking at me. There's no reason to pick a fight with someone who does you no harm.

Wouldn't it be nice, Vinnie, if someday dogs and cats, and cats and birds, and all the other animals who fight each other could just lay aside their animosity and learn to get along with each other?

It sure would make for a more peaceful world, boss. To tell you the truth, I often dream of that day when we could all be friends and not have to fight each other.

That's a beautiful dream, Vinnie. Do you think it will ever come true?

That's a good question, boss. You and I may not live long enough to see it happen, but that shouldn't keep us from dreaming about it and hoping it might happen someday.

I don't know, Vinnie. That may be one of those impossible dreams that will never come true.

I hope you're wrong, boss, but that won't keep me from holding on to my dream.

Maybe you're a hopeless dreamer, Vinnie.

Maybe boss, but if you don't have a dream, how will your dreams comes true?

You've been listening to <u>South Pacific</u> again, haven't you Vinnie?

You caught me, boss, and if you play your cards right, I'll sing it for you.

Reflection:
1. What dreams do I have for my life?
2. What dreams do I have for my family and friends?
3. What dreams do I have for the world?

Nobody can appreciate Christmas if they don't
have the heart of a child.

MARILYN ICSMAN

FOURTH SUNDAY OF ADVENT

Matthew 1:18-24

The story of the events leading to the birth of Jesus reveals the dilemma faced by Jesus' parents. Basically, it was a question of both parents trusting in the message God revealed to them through the agency of angels. Mary trusted that the birth of her child would occur through the power of the Holy Spirit. Joseph too had to trust that the child Mary was carrying was indeed the work of God. For Joseph it was necessary, because without that trust, his trust in Mary would have been destroyed and his hope for a successful marriage would have ended. The story of Joseph's dilemma is a timely reminder of the importance of trust in any successful relationship.

DO NOT OPEN!

Is that the Christmas tree you're carrying down the steps, boss?

That's right, Vinnie. Christmas is just around the corner.

I can hardly wait, boss. I love Christmas.

Me too, Vinnie. I love the Christmas carols and the excitement of the children. I love the Christmas decorations and the peaceful quiet of sitting near the fire on a winter's evening, watching the lights on the tree and just thinking about Christmas and what it means.

I love all those things too, boss, but you left out one of the best parts.

What did I forget, Vinnie?

You forgot the presents. I love all the presents people bring for me.

Yes, I guess that's an important part of Christmas too. Sometimes I forget that you never stopped being like a little child looking for presents at Christmas.

That's not a fault, boss. Nobody can appreciate Christmas if they don't have the heart of a child.

You're absolutely right, Vinnie. That's why I enjoy watching you at Christmas. You remind me of what it means to be like a little child.

So, boss, when you get the tree up, will you start putting all the presents people bring us under the tree?

Presuming that there will be presents this year, yes. I will put some of them under the tree until we get a chance to open them on Christmas day.

That's great, boss, and don't worry, I'm sure there will be some presents for us, but what do you mean "some of them"?

For sure, I'll put my presents under the tree, but I may not want to put your presents there until Christmas day.

Why would you do a thing like that, boss? I enjoy looking at all the nice wrappings and the ribbon.

I've also noticed, Vinnie, that you enjoy sniffing the packages to find out which ones belong to you.

What's wrong with that, boss? It's just a little natural curiosity. That's part of what makes Christmas so much fun.

That's true, Vinnie, but I'm not so sure I can trust you to wait until Christmas. Sometimes your interest in food transcends your will power.

How could you say a thing like that, boss?

I hate to say it, but I guess I just don't trust you.

Put the presents out, boss. You can trust me.

Reflection:
1. Are there times that I fail to place my trust completely in God?
2. Are there some people I find it hard to trust? Is that distrust warranted?
3. Am I a person others can trust?

I've also noticed, Vinnie, that you enjoy sniffing the packages
to find out which ones belong to you.   DALTON CRESSWELL

CHRISTMAS SEASON

CHRISTMAS
Luke 2:1-14

Christmas is so beautiful, and everybody enjoys cele-brating Christmas, even those who do not believe in Christ. For some Christmas is a time to share warmth and good feelings with family and friends.. For those with the gift of faith, it is so much more. For them it is the pledge of God's never ending love for humanity and the world we live in. It is the realization that the promise of Jesus to be with us always is being kept. We set up our Christmas trees, decorate our homes with light, and place the cribs on our mantles to bring to mind our belief that Jesus is the Light of the World. He will be with us throughout the years to come.

RISE UP SHEPHERDS

My goodness, you frightened me Vinnie. What are you doing up here at this hour of the morning? It's only 1:30!

I had to come up and make sure you were still here, boss. I was having a really strange dream, and I wanted to share it with you.

Do you remember what was your dream was about, Vinnie?

Yes. I was standing in the middle of a large field on a very bright, starlit night.

Were you all by yourself, or was I with you?

I'm getting to that, boss. But first let me tell you what happened.

I'm listening, Vinnie. Go ahead.

I wasn't exactly all by myself, but I was the only dog there, with a whole lot of sheep.

That's strange, isn't it Vinnie?

I thought so, boss. After all, I'm not a sheep dog.

No you surely aren't, Vinnie.

So, there I was, standing with all those sheep, when all of a sudden I hear this beautiful music.

You mean the kind you hear when I turn on my radio?

A little like that, boss, but this was much more beautiful. There seemed to be thousands of voices, and they filled the sky with their singing. It was heavenly.

So tell me, Vinnie, what happened next?

There were these men there. They seemed to be in charge of the sheep, and I heard them talking to each other. They were saying they ought to go over to see what was happening.

So what did you do, Vinnie?

I followed them of course. I was curious too.

And what did you find, Vinnie.

It's hard to put into words, boss, it was so wonderful. We went into a kind of cave and there we found a beautiful young woman with her husband and their baby—a newborn baby. And the music just kept getting more and more beautiful.

Gosh, Vinnie. That sounds great. I wish I had been with you.

That's why I'm here, boss. I wanted to see if you were here, so I could take you to see it for yourself.

Thanks, Vinnie. I appreciate your concern. But do you really think I can enter into your dream?

You can if you want, boss, you can if you want.

Reflection:
1. What are my special Christmas traditions?
2. What is my favorite thing about Christmas?
3. How does Christmas strengthen my belief in God's never-ending love?

That's great, boss, and don't worry, I'm sure there will be some presents for us, but what do you mean "some of them"?   ANTHONY GRETHER

FEAST OF THE HOLY FAMILY

Luke 2: 41-52

Each year we recall the Holy Family of Nazareth. We are reminded that their life was like ours in many respects. We appreciate that the Holy Family had problems, just as our families do. They were poor and in times of greatest stress, they experienced homelessness. They lived among strangers for a time before they could return to their own home. When Joseph died, Mary was left without a spouse and Jesus was left without a father. Later, Mary would suffer the loss of a friend. The trials of the Holy Family are a source of inspiration and strength for our families, as we experience problems and setbacks.

FAMILY MATTERS

So, Vinnie, did you have a nice Christmas?
I think so, boss. I received a lot of nice treats, for which I am always grateful, and I enjoyed all the beautiful singing I heard drifting over from the church. And speaking of the church, I thought it looked just beautiful with all the flowers and trees and especially the

crib. All in all, boss, I would say it was a beautiful Christmas. Having said that, boss, I confess I was a little concerned about you.

You were?

Yes, one night, not long before Christmas, I heard some commotion up in your room and I went up to see what the matter was. You seemed to be in some distress, so I waited for a while on the steps, and then I decided there was nothing I could do, so I went downstairs again.

Yes, I saw you Vinnie, and you were right about not being able to help, but I appreciated your concern.

I've been thinking about that, boss, and I realized it is part of being part of a family. I am part of a family, aren't I?

Absolutely, Vinnie. Everybody knows that.

Well, when you're part of a family, boss, you have people to worry about other than yourself.

That's true, Vinnie. Sometimes family life is filled with many joys and we can be happy together. But then things happen, like sickness, and we all have to try to get through it together. That's what families are for, because nobody wants to be alone, especially when they are suffering.

You know, boss, I think that happens in every family, even God's family.

Why do you say that, Vinnie?

I remember that story you told me about Jesus' family and how they had to leave their home and travel hundreds of miles to a foreign land because Herod was trying to kill the baby. That must have been very difficult for them, but they were a family and they did it together.

That's a good point, Vinnie. That's why the Holy Family is a good example for us. Every family has problems, but if we stay together, we can overcome them.

Well, we got through this crisis together, boss, and I'm glad to see you up and about again.

Me too, Vinnie. Now we can get back to helping other families who are having problems like we had.

Reflection:
1. What problems has our family experienced?
2. In what way are they similar to the problems of the Holy Family?
3. How did the Holy Family find strength to endure their trials?

EPIPHANY

Matthew 2:1-12

FOLLOW YOUR STAR

The three Wise Men are called "wise" for a reason. They were obviously blessed with the many things we desire on earth. The very fact they were able to make such a journey tells us that they were wealthy—maybe even kings. But they understood that money could not purchase what they were seeking. There is so much more to happiness than acquiring more things. This is a timely reminder, coming to us after the frenzy of shopping we have just experienced. Now it is time to get down to the serious pursuit of the gift which will bring us just what we always wanted.

Hello, Vinnie. Where have you been?

I was over in the dining room resting.

So what brings you into the kitchen at this time?

I've been waiting, boss.

I've been working out here for quite a while. It's strange that you should appear right at this moment, Vinnie. Is there something I can do for you?

Not exactly, boss. I've just been waiting until now, because I didn't see any reason to come to the kitchen before.

Sometimes I think you sit out there in the dining room, just sniffing at the different odors that come from the kitchen, and then, when you smell something that attracts your attention, you make your move.

You're very perceptive, boss. That's exactly how it works. You see, it's a very delicate art to be able to distinguish the smells from one another and choose only the one that is going to lead to pay dirt.

Not being blessed with the sensitive nose you have, Vinnie, I have never been able to make those distinctions.

I can understand that well enough, boss, but I think you people do the same sort of thing, using the senses that serve you best.

Now that you mention it, Vinnie, I think you're right. I suppose we use the gift of sight in the same way you use the gift of smell. We tend to pursue those things which are most pleasing to the eye, just as you choose things that are most pleasing to the nose.

That's true, boss, but I don't think you understand completely yet.

What am I missing, Vinnie?

You're aiming too low, boss. Your best gift is not seeing, but rather understanding. It's one thing to see with your eyes; it's even more important to understand with your mind. That's where you have it way over on me.

I get it, Vinnie. Yes, you're right! For us, it's important to distinguish the things that will really make us happy, using the gift of our intellect, just the way you use your nose.

That's right, boss. It's what we dogs call, "following your star."

Dogs call it that too, Vinnie? I thought we were the only ones who used that phrase.

Oh no, boss! It goes way back. Wise men have always followed the one star that can lead them to what they are searching for. Too many stars are dead ends. They can learn from us dogs not to follow after stars that will bring them only false rewards.

Reflection:
1. What is the most important thing I can do with me life?
2. Does my life revolve around this goal?
3. Is there something directing my life other than what I consider really important?

BAPTISM OF JESUS

Matthew 3:13-17

From the time we were conceived, God had a plan for us. We were created for a purpose. We were to be part of the ongoing creation of the world, doing our part to advance the Kingdom of God on earth. God knew from all eternity what our purpose would be, but we must wait to discover that purpose in our life. When we finally understand what our vocation is, we begin to live a new and satisfying life, filled with purpose and meaning. In a way, that search never ends, as we discover the "call within a call." Each day we pray that God will show us how to best serve Him "this day."

ACCEPTING THE CALL

Vinnie, do you know that you celebrate your birthday this month?

No, I didn't know that, boss. What day is my birthday?

It's on the 22nd of this month, and you're going to be 9 years old.

That sure sounds old, doesn't it, boss? It seems like just yesterday that I came here as a little puppy.

Can you remember that day, Vinnie?

I sure can, boss. It was a cold morning and there was snow on the ground. I was so small and my legs were so short that I had a hard time hopping through the snow.

That's right, Vinnie. You were so small that I could hold you in the palm of my hand.

I remember that, boss. You put me up on the step at the back of the house to take my picture.

I did that because there was snow on the step and that way I could see you. You were just a little black bundle of fur.

That was a long time ago, boss, and these past nine years have gone so quickly.

Looking back, Vinnie, would you say that day was the most important day of your life?

Without a doubt, boss. That was the day I began my life as a church dog.

I suppose you would have to say that the day you were born was also important, don't you think, Vinnie?

Sure, boss, that was an important day too, but the day they brought me to St. Vincent was like being born all over again, and this time it was even more important.

Why do you say that, Vinnie?

Because, boss, on that day I understood what my life was for. Those first few weeks of my life were good, but I didn't really know what I was supposed to do. Up until the day I came to St. Vincent, I led just a dog's life, but then I came here and began my life's work as a church dog.

That's true, Vinnie. Your life really began on the day I received a call asking if I wanted you.

Funny you should put it that way, boss.

What do you mean, Vinnie?

You said you received a call, but really it was I that received a call.

You did?

Sure, that was the day I received the call to work for God. I guess you could say it was my baptism day.

Reflection:
1. When was I first aware of God's call in my life?
2. How did God's call come to me?
3. How did my life change on the day I knew my call from God?

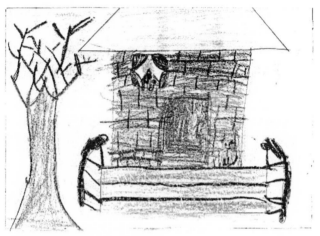

You put me up on the step at the back of
the house to take my picture.

COLLEEN GOETZ

LENTEN SEASON

FIRST SUNDAY OF LENT
Genesis 2:7-9; 3:1-7

Temptations are common to everyone who aspires to a spiritual life. Those who seek to follow in the footsteps of Jesus will not be exempt, since Jesus himself was subject to temptation. When Adam was confronted by God and asked if he had eaten of the forbidden fruit, Adam tried to evade God's judgment by blaming his sin on Eve, who in turn, blamed the serpent. We are all children of our first parents and we all follow the same road, trying to blame our faults on others. Lent is a time for us to face honestly the sins of which we are guilty, repent of them, and turn back to God. In this season of prayer and penance, we prepare for the gift of new life at Easter.

GAINS AND LOSSES

What are you doing, boss?
I'm feeling for your ribs, Vinnie.
What's wrong with my ribs, boss?

There's nothing wrong with them, Vinnie, it's just that I can't find them.

You mean I've lost my ribs!

No, Vinnie, I'm sure you haven't lost them, but they seem to be pretty well hidden under a lot of other stuff.

Is that a problem, boss?

It says in this morning's paper that if you can't feel your dog's ribs, it means he's too fat.

In that case, boss, we've got a problem.

Yes, Vinnie, I think we do, but it isn't something we can't take care of.

What's this "we" you're talking about, boss? It sounds to me like this is something I'm going to have to take care of.

You're right about that, Vinnie, and the first step is for you to admit that you eat too much.

Now wait just a small minute, boss. It isn't my fault.

Well if it isn't your fault, then whose fault is it?

It's all those people who keep giving me treats. If they would just stop feeding me, I wouldn't have a problem.

Hold on there, Vinnie. I think you're overlooking something.

What's that, boss?

I've seen the way you act around certain people. You've got them wrapped around your little toe.

I have no idea of what you're talking about, boss.

Oh yes you do, Vinnie. You sit there with that "poor, pitiful Pearl" look and pretend that you haven't eaten in weeks. Then, just to emphasize the point, you put your paw up on them to let them know this is serious.

Gosh, boss, I didn't know you saw that, but you have to admit that it's pretty effective.

That's the problem, Vinnie, it's very effective, and as a result you end up eating much more than you should. That's why I can't feel your ribs: too many treats equals too much fat.

All right, boss, you're on to my tricks. Maybe I'm going to have to take responsibility for this padding around my ribs.

That's right, Vinnie. It does no good to blame others for your faults. Once you admit to them, then you're on the road to recovery.

If I admit it, boss, would you let me have a biscuit?

Reflection:
1. What are my worst temptations?
2. How can I fight these temptations during Lent?
3. What is my goal for this Lent?

You're right about that, Vinnie, and the first step is for you to admit that you eat too much.   CHRIS MAXIMOVICH

SECOND SUNDAY OF LENT

Matthew 17:1-9

The transfiguration of Jesus on Mt. Tabor revealed him as the Son of God. It was a vision the apostles never forgot. The apostles wanted Jesus to remain with them on that holy mountain—it was almost like being in heaven. But that was not to be; not until Jesus had endured his passion and death on the cross. Then and only then would they truly know and understand the kind of messiah Jesus was. So too, we must be willing to endure life's sufferings, if we are to share in the glory of heaven. We will be transformed, but only if we are willing to die with him and then rise with him.

JUST LIKE NEW

What happened to you, Vinnie? You look so much better.

I should look better, boss, I've just been given a bath.

Well good for you, Vinnie. You're clean and shining like the noon day sun.

Thanks, boss, I'm glad you noticed.

I remember my first dog, Timmie. She absolutely hated getting a bath. All I had to do is mention the word to her and she would put her ears down, her tail between her legs, and walk away from me as fast as she could.

Some dogs are like that, boss, and to tell you the truth, taking a bath is not at the top of my list of things I like to do.

But I've watched you, Vinnie. When Karen mentions bath to you, you march right up the steps in front of her and step into the tub as if you actually enjoyed it

It may appear that way, boss, but that's not the way it is. I do all those things, because I know it's something I'm going to have to do, so I may as well get it over with.

I wonder why dogs have such a difficult time taking a bath, Vinnie. It doesn't seem like such a bad thing to do.

I think you would understand a little better, boss, if you were a dog. You see we dogs are always afraid of getting something in our ears or in our eyes, and that soapy bath water can really be a problem. On top of that, it's rather embarrassing to be hosed down, and that soap can smell pretty bad. The whole thing is just not very attractive.

But you do it anyway, Vinnie, without making a fuss the way Timmie did.

The way I see it, boss, it's the price I have to pay for the results you mentioned. When it's all over, I feel clean and my coat is shining and bright. I look like a new dog and I even feel like a new dog.

Yes, you do, Vinnie. You're completely transformed. I'm afraid to take you out in public, because all the women are going to go crazy over you.

That's it, boss. You've hit on another reason I submit to taking a bath. The rewards are very gratifying.

I'm beginning to understand, Vinnie. Actually, you like the results of the bath even though you don't like taking a bath.

I guess you could say that, boss. You see, I've learned that being made new again exacts a price. Taking a bath is only the means that leads to living a whole new life.

Reflection:

1. Have I ever experienced the feeling of being renewed?
2. Was there a price to be paid for that feeling?
3. Is there a demand at present which calls me to a new life?

THIRD SUNDAY OF LENT

John 4:5-42

There were many reasons Jesus would not be talking with the woman at the well: she was a woman in a culture where women were not recognized as equals; she was a gentile, and Jews did not speak easily with gentiles; she was a Samaritan , and we all know what Jews thought of Samaritans. But Jesus did speak with this woman, and in doing so he revealed her soul and she became one of those who spread the story of Jesus to others. Differences and disagreements persist in our world, sometimes becoming like walls which divide. Jesus teaches us to transcend those walls in order to bring them down. In the end we are all children of God, and brothers and sister to one another. A friendly hello can go a long way to making peace.

LET'S TALK

Calm down, Vinnie. What are you so excited about?

Let me out, boss. There's somebody out in the courtyard. I've got to check it out.

All right, just calm down. I'm moving as fast as I can.

Knock, knock.

Don't tell me you want to come in already.

Yes, boss, our visitor disappeared.

From the smell of things, Vinnie, you're lucky he did. Do you know what was out there, Vinnie?

I'm not sure, boss. I think it was a cat, but I'm not sure. It looked a little like a cat, but it had a strange looking stripe down its back. I don't think I've ever seen a cat that looked like that.

No, you haven't, Vinnie. That wasn't a cat you heard out there, it was a skunk, and you're lucky it disappeared before you found it.

Why do you say that, boss? What's wrong with a skunk? I think he looked rather cute.

He may have looked cute, but skunks have a very unusual way of defending themselves.

What do they do, boss?

They release a very foul smelling spray, and if it gets on you, I would have to take you to the basement and wash you in tomato juice, and when you dried you would look like I had given you a spiked hairdo.

That sounds terrible, boss. Would you really have to go to all that trouble?

I'm afraid I would, Vinnie.

But, boss, what if the skunk and I got along with each other and the skunk didn't have to spray me?

That doesn't sound very likely to me, Vinnie, not the way you go flying out of the house barking like the house is on fire. You're enough to scare anybody or anything.

Ah, but boss, you underestimate me. I have ways of dealing with things like these skunks you're talking about.

And what would that be, Vinnie?

It's easy, boss. You just walk up to them and introduce yourself, and after a few pleasantries, you start talking with them in a friendly fashion. You ask them where they live and how are their children, and things like that. Before you know it, you've struck up a relationship and there's no need to get defensive.

That's good, Vinnie. Do you think it would work?

It always works, boss. If you treat others as friends, most often you'll find they really are.

Reflection:
1. Are there some people I have trouble relating to?
2. What causes this difficulty?
3. Have I ever reached out to someone I felt uncomfortable with?

FOURTH SUNDAY OF LENT

1 Samuel 16:1b, 6-7

Sent to Jesse's house to anoint the future king, the prophet Samuel selects the one who appears most kingly. None of the seven older sons of Jesse are the ones God had in mind. It was the youngest son, David. God explains to the prophet that God sees differently than we might see. In the gospel, Jesus gives sight to the man born blind. In time the man comes to understand more clearly who Jesus is. Getting to know Jesus and getting to know others as God knows them takes time. Outward appearances and behavior can be deceptive. Jesus gives us the sight which helps us to see people as God sees them.

I CAN SEE CLEARLY NOW

What's the rush, Vinnie, you're practically pulling me over?

Up there, boss, don't you see?

I see a woman walking two dogs, but I don't see any reason to go running after them. As a matter of fact, it looks to me like that woman is speeding up in an effort to steer clear of us.

That may be, boss, but I've go to catch up with those two dogs before she gets away from us.

I'm surprised you even saw those dogs, Vinnie. At times it seems you don't see very much at all.

Oh, I can see what I need to see, boss. I can spot a chipmunk from a hundred yards.

That's what I call selective seeing, Vinnie. You see only the things your interested in.

I suppose you're right about that, boss, but there's more to it than that.

Like what?

Well, I can see them from here all right, but I really don't know much about them. I've got to get up close to find out what kind of dogs they are.

I can tell you that, Vinnie. One is large and the other one is small.

Brilliant, boss! I can see that, but is the small one friendly or not; and is the large one all bark and no bite? You see not all dogs are the same. Each one has its own personality, and sometimes seeing a dog doesn't tell you all you need to know. Sometimes a dog's behavior betrays the real dog that lies beneath.

That helps me to understand something, Vinnie.

What's that, boss?

A little way back, that small dog came flying at us like he was ready to tear us to pieces. If he hadn't come to a screeching halt in front of the fence, there's no telling what he might have done. But you didn't even flinch. You acted as if he weren't even there.

First of all, boss, it was a she not a he, and besides that, I know that dog. We've seen her before.

I know we have, but that didn't stop her from rushing at us.

You misunderstood her, boss. She wasn't out to get us. She was just happy to see us again, and wanted to come and say "hello."

She could have fooled me, Vinnie.

Just stay with me, boss, someday you'll see things the way they really are.

Reflection:

1. Do I misjudge people because of their appearance or be because they act differently?
2. Maybe I can learn to see people the way God sees them.
3. How can I get to see and know Jesus more clearly?

FIFTH SUNDAY OF LENT

John 11: 1-45

The story of the raising of Lazarus can be read on different levels. It surely is written to strengthen our faith in our own resurrection. Perhaps we might also read it to help us through those times in our lives when we feel less than fully alive. As a result of sickness or personal loss, we may experience depression and fear; it is as if the darkness of death enters our life. Through these experiences we grow to understand the place of suffering in our lives. The raising of Lazarus gives us assurance that Jesus can lift us up to a life we never knew before. We need the courage to "take away the stone"; trusting that Jesus can restore the life we have lost.

JUST LIKE NEW

How much longer is this Lent going to last, boss? Why do you ask, Vinnie?

Oh, you know, I was just wondering. I find myself getting hungry more than I used to.

You'll be happy to know, Vinnie, that we have only two more weeks.

That sounds like a long time to me, boss. I was hoping to get back to my regular diet. I've noticed that I'm not getting quite as much food in my bowl as I normally do.

That's true, Vinnie. You've been doing a little fasting for Lent. I thought it might do you good.

Why would you say that, boss? How can eating less do me any good? I think it's very difficult.

As I've told you before, Vinnie, there's more to life than eating.

Yes, I've heard you tell me that, boss, but I find that easy to forget. Eating is right at the top of my favorite things list.

I know, Vinnie, and that's the reason I thought you might derive some benefit from doing a little fasting during Lent. Your eating has caused you to put on more weight than is good for you. I was hoping you might lose a few pounds.

I suppose that wouldn't hurt me, boss, but it sure is hard.

It's supposed to be hard, Vinnie. Sometimes important things come only by hard work, and fasting is hard work.

You can say that again, boss, and I'm afraid I have to agree with you that I am better off without all that weight.

I'm glad to hear that, Vinnie. Does that mean you've noticed a change in your life?

I sure have, boss. Haven't you noticed it also?

Maybe I have, but why don't you tell me about it?

The best way to describe it, boss, is that I feel so much younger. I can run faster, chase after things more quickly, and breathe more easily. I feel like I've received a whole new life.

That's great, Vinnie. I was hoping you would feel that way, and now that you mention it, I have noticed that you're acting more like you did when you were a puppy.

Well, I'm not a puppy anymore, but all this fasting has paid off and I am enjoying life more than ever. Thanks for the help, boss, I wouldn't have done it without you.

You're welcome, Vinnie. It's good to see you having a good time again.

Reflection:
1. Try to recall times when you experienced pain and sadness in your life.
2. What were the circumstances that caused this?
3. How did God lift you from these times to happier times in your life?

PALM SUNDAY
OF THE LORD'S PASSION

Matthew 26:14—27:66

The story of Our Lord's passion and death are said to be the first chapters to be written of the gospels as we now know them. This is understandable, considering the tremendous impact this event must have had on the initial followers of Jesus, and the fact that all that we believe concerning him flows from his passion, death and resurrection. Reading the entire account of the passion and death of Jesus, as we do at the beginning of Holy Week, cannot help but remind us of the core message of this chapter in the life of Our Lord. While each of the details in the passion narrative is matter for reflection, the over-arching message is unmistakable. Jesus laid down his life for us. There is no greater proof of his love for us. No other proof is necessary.

WHAT A FRIEND

Where are we going today, boss?

We'll go on our usual Wednesday walk through the neighborhood. Is that all right with you?

Any walk is all right with me, boss, but I do have a special love for that particular walk.

Why is that, Vinnie?

I meet a lot of interesting dogs on that walk. It seems that the people who live in that part of the city have dogs to walk, just like you and me. I enjoy seeing all of them and exchanging sniffs.

Yes, that's true, Vinnie, and being as friendly as you are, you don't miss a one.

No offense, boss, but sometimes I get a bit tired of hanging out with people like yourself, so it's refreshing for me to get out and see some of my own people. You know, the four footed kind who speak my language.

I think I can understand that, Vinnie. We have saying to express that: "birds of a feather flock together."

That's it exactly, boss. I guess you people are a lot like us in that respect.

I'd say we are, Vinnie, but we also have to be careful not to let that go too far. Like you, we find it important also to learn how to get along with those who are not "of our feather."

Let me ask you something, Vinnie.

Shoot, boss.

On the walk we are taking today there are two really large Dobermans that come sailing out at us as if they are ready to give us what for. I've often wondered what would happen to me if they jumped over that fence.

First of all, boss, your worries are unfounded. Those dogs used to be guard dogs or police dogs, but now their aggressiveness has been bred out of them and they are very good family dogs.

I'm happy to hear that, Vinnie. It's just that they are so much larger than you and seem to be so muscular. I know that you can stand up to them bark to bark, but how would you fare if you were to get into it together?

I can't say for sure, boss. They are stronger than I, and I'm not really the fighting kind, but I would do what I have to do.

Do you realize you could get hurt or even killed?

Yes, boss, but if worse came to worse, I would do what I could to save you.

Thanks, Vinnie. It's hard to find friends like you.

Reflection:
1. Take the time to read one of the four passion narratives slowly and reflectively.
2. How does this affect you?
3. For whom am I ready to lay down my life?

GRACIE DAVIS

EASTER SEASON

EASTER SUNDAY
Matthew 28:1-10

The Resurrection of Jesus is a pledge of our own resurrection. Just as Jesus has risen, so shall we. The gift of everlasting life promised by Jesus finds its fulfillment in heaven, but it begins here on earth. The gift of life comes from our faith in Jesus, and when we have accepted him in our life, we begin to experience a new life we've never known before. This new life fills us with purpose and gives us meaning. If we were lost, not knowing what our life was for, we discover, as Jesus did, that our life is "for others." Self-interest begins to fade and each day is a new day to be spent giving to others; and in the giving to find we have everything.

NEW LIFE

Hey boss, isn't this the neighborhood Cheriese used to live in?

Cheriese who?

My goodness, boss, I knew you were getting older, but don't you remember? She's the young woman we found freezing one morning when we were opening the church.

Oh yes, of course, I remember her very well. You and I saved her life. I was told if we hadn't found her when we did, she would have frozen to death. As it was, she suffered severe frostbite and spent several weeks in the hospital. So then, Vinnie, what was your question?

I was asking if this is where Cheriese used to live.

Yes, Vinnie, you're absolutely right. This is where she lived. Why do you ask?

It's just that I've been thinking about her lately and wondered what ever happened to her. Do you know?

It's funny you should ask, Vinnie. As a matter of fact I received a letter from her just this morning.

So tell me, boss, what did she have to say?

She told me she has been saved.

What does that mean, boss?

It means that she has turned her life over to Jesus, and now she is trying to put her life back in order.

That's good, boss. She was having some problems when we found her, wasn't she, boss?

Yes she was, Vinnie. She was hanging out with the wrong people and she was involved with drinking and drugs. That's why she ended up on our lawn. One of her friends beat her up and left her there.

That's terrible, boss. Is she going to be all right now?

She's made a good start, Vinnie, and she says in her letter that she has five months of sobriety under her belt, but she needs to stay on the program to avoid going back to her old habits.

I hope she can stay with it, boss. Maybe she can help others, using her experience to convince them to stay away from all that stuff.

That's exactly what she wants to do, Vinnie. She says that when she has herself straightened out, she wants to help young people, so they don't end up the way she did.

That's a great story, boss. It sounds to me like Cheriese has found a whole new life. She's risen up, just like Jesus.

Reflection:
1. Have I ever experienced my relationship to Jesus as a source of new life?
2. What are the signs of everlasting life present to me now?
3. Do I pray for the faith to believe in everlasting life in heaven?

WILL HORN

SECOND SUNDAY OF EASTER

John 20:19-31

SEEING IS BELIEVING

These are times when many find their traditional beliefs being challenged by the findings of science, which seem to negate the need for the existence of God. Scientists, in their search for the origins of our world and our species, are unable to incorporate faith into their analysis, since faith is not subject to the scientific method. Both science and faith have their respective places, and as believers we are constantly challenged to reaffirm our faith in a personal God who stands behind all the discoveries we make. Compounding our problem is the fact that so many others seem to have lost their faith in God, leaving us to wonder if we are the only ones who don't "get it."

I see you sitting there, Vinnie. Is there something you wanted?

It's nearly 7:30 in the morning, boss. Haven't you forgotten something?

Not that I'm aware of. What did you have in mind?

It may not seem important to you, boss, but I was in the kitchen just now, and I noticed my food dish was empty.

I could have told you that, Vinnie. I haven't filled it yet this morning.

That's what I was worried about. I was beginning to wonder if you might have forgotten.

Now Vinnie! How could you ever think a thing like that? You know that I have filled your food dish every morning since you came here.

I'm sorry about that, boss. I guess it's just a dog thing.

What's that supposed to mean?

It's like this, boss. Most dogs have to go out looking for food every day. We don't ordinarily have someone giving us food, so we have to go look for it.

But you're not like the other dogs, Vinnie. You have someone to take care of you and give you food.

Yes, I know that, boss, but when I see all the other dogs who don't know there is someone like you, I find myself starting to think as they do and wondering if you're still going to feed me.

I can understand that, Vinnie. I guess we all have trouble holding on to our hopes when it seems everyone else has abandoned them.

I'm glad to hear you say that, boss.

So, are you a believer now, even though your bowl is empty?

Maybe. I'll have to wait and see.

What do you mean, you'll have to wait and see?

Hey boss, the dish is still empty. I know you're telling me to be patient and wait for you to fill it, but I'm the kind of dog who wants a little more to go on than just the things you're telling me.

What more do you need, Vinnie? It seems my word ought to be enough for you.

It may seem that way, boss, but I'll be convinced when I can see that the dish is full and I can smell the sweet odor of real food wafting from my bowl.

You ask a lot, Vinnie, but come on, let's go get your breakfast, so you can get over your doubts.

Ah, I'm beginning to catch the sweet smells already.

Reflection:

1. Do I find myself tempted to abandon my faith because so many others have done so?
2. Do the findings of science cause me to wonder about my faith?
3. How can I strengthen my faith in the face of so many temptations to question it?

THIRD SUNDAY OF EASTER

Luke 24:12-35

The story of the two disciples on the road to Emmaus is one of the most beautiful in the Bible. It teaches us that Jesus has not abandoned us, but that he walks with us on our life's journey. Sometimes we are too busy to notice his presence, but he is always there waiting for us in the Scriptures we meditate on and the celebration of the Eucharist we share with one another. With all the devices available to us, we become very adept at managing our time, but good time management makes room for an "appointment with Jesus" every day. We must never walk so fast as to lose sight of the Lord.

JUST A CLOSER WALK

Are you ready, Vinnie? It's time for our walk.
Like a battery, boss, I'm ever ready.
For a dog your age, you still have a lot of life left in you, Vinnie. I'll tell you what. Since you're so sharp, why don't you choose the route today?

Thanks, boss. I really appreciate that. I'll tell you where I would like to go. I love those walks we take when I don't need a leash. Can we do that today?

Sure, I know just the place. It's a little out of town and there is plenty of land for you to run and hunt. I think you're going to enjoy it.

Sounds good to me, boss. Let's get moving.

Here we are, Vinnie. You can run to your heart's content, and I'll just walk around with you.

Hang on, boss, I'm really going to enjoy this. See you later.

Have fun Vinnie, I'll be right behind you.

Hmmm, I wonder where the boss went. He said he would be right behind me, but I don't see him anywhere. Oh well, he'll catch up with me, I have more work to do. I think that's a fresh squirrel trail I smell. I'd better check it out. Uh-huh, just as I thought, it leads to another tree. No problem, there are other scents to pursue. I wonder what happened to the boss. I seem to have lost him.

Look at that Vinnie out there. He's having such a good time; he doesn't even know I'm here. It's good to see him enjoying himself, but I know before long he's going to know I'm missing, and he'll come running back to greet me.

I ought to go looking for the boss, but wait a minute. Is that a deer scent I'm smelling? Oh, this is just too good. I've got to check it out. Whew, I'm getting tired. Those deer can cover a lot of ground in a very short time. I think I'm getting too old for this sort of thing. Maybe I'd better go back and find the boss. He's a little slow and probably wondering where I am.

Oh, there you are, boss. I thought I was going to have trouble finding you.

No, Vinnie, I've been here the whole time. You were just too busy to notice.

It's good to see you, boss. Come on, you can walk me home.

Reflection:

1. When am I most conscious of the Lord's presence in my life?
2. Do I pray the scriptures, looking to see the Lord in my daily life?
3. Am I faithful in looking for Jesus by celebrating the Eucharist together with them regularly?

FOURTH SUNDAY OF EASTER

John 10:1-10

One of the most endearing and enduring images of Christ is that of the "Good Shepherd." This description of the relationship we have with the Lord helps us to appreciate the importance of knowing that Jesus is always with us. Sometimes he is the shepherd who goes looking for the sheep that has strayed; at other times he is the shepherd whose voice calls to us in times of trouble and distress to save and comfort us. Most of all, the Good Shepherd is the one who loves us and wants always to remain close to us.

LIKE A SHEPHERD

Slow down, Vinnie, what's your hurry?
Something up ahead has caught my interest, boss.

I could tell, Vinnie, but what is it?

I think there's another dog ahead of us on the trail. I can see its boss is holding onto its leash, just as you are mine. I want to catch up to make my acquaintance with them.

That's a good idea, Vinnie, but I think you're going to be surprised, because I don't think that's a dog he's holding onto.

Well, let's get going, boss, so I can find out.

Okay, I'm coming.

I think you may be right this time, boss. I don't think it's a dog at all, it's a little boy.

I could have told you that, Vinnie, but I wanted you to find out for yourself, since you never seem to listen to me.

But why would he have his little son on a leash, boss? I thought leashes were only for dogs.

They are, Vinnie. Look a little closer.

Now I see. That's not a leash. The father is holding on to his son's hand. What's wrong, boss, can't the little guy walk without holding on to something?

Let's think about that, Vinnie. Can you think of any other reasons his father may be holding his hand?

Now that you mention it, boss, I suppose it may be to keep his son from wandering off and getting lost.

That's a good point, Vinnie. Sometimes children get distracted and the next thing you know, they've lost their parents. That's when they need help.

Of course that would never happen to me, boss. But you've told me before that I have this leash to keep me out of trouble with speeding cars and buses. Maybe the father is holding on to his son's hand to keep him from getting hurt.

True, Vinnie. There aren't any speeding cars down here on the trail, but there is a river down below, and that could be dangerous.

Those are all good reasons, aren't they, boss? But I can think of an even better reason.

What's that, Vinnie?

That father really loves his son and holding on to his hand is how he shows his love.

That's great, Vinnie. Now I think you've got it.

Reflection:

1. Through the Sacrament of Reconciliation do I seek frequently to heed the voice of Jesus calling me from a sinful habit?

2. Do I listen in prayer to the voice of Jesus in times of trouble?

3. Am I aware of the many ways in which Jesus remains close to me each day?

THE FIFTH SUNDAY OF EASTER

John 14:1-12

Jesus tells Thomas that he is "the way and the truth and the life." It may be more understandable to read this threefold description of Jesus backwards. It is the fullness of life we all seek. This fullness results not only in living a good and meaningful life on earth, but also the promise of everlasting life in heaven. Life on this earth is a great blessing, which we should treasure more and more each day, but ultimately earthly life fails to satisfy our deepest yearning for participation in a higher life, which draws us beyond ourselves to sharing in the very life of God. Jesus is the true way to finding that life. By accepting Jesus as our role model, we discover the life we are looking for, even if it means losing the life we have on earth.

WAY TO GO

What day is it, boss?

Today is Thursday, Vinnie. Why do you ask?

I was just wondering what route our walk is taking us today.

Do you mean to tell me you know what route goes with each day?

Of course I do, boss. You're such a creature of habit that it didn't take me long to figure out exactly where our walk would take us. After all, you've been taking the same route for the past eight years. Monday is Highland Square, Wednesday is Memorial Parkway, Thursday is the towpath, etc. I've got them all memorized.

That's pretty good, Vinnie. You know more than I give you credit for.

That's true, boss. But I must confess I don't understand why we must follow the same route each day. Why not try a little variety?

That's a good question, Vinnie, and there are three reasons for doing it the way we do.

Okay, boss, go ahead and impress me.

First, these are all good walks.

What's so good about them? As far as I'm concerned a walk is a walk.

I suppose you could say that, Vinnie, but I like a walk that's interesting. It's easy to get tired of taking walks, unless there's an opportunity to see new things and new people.

I guess you have a point there, boss. Today we met that little boy who wondered if it was all right to pet me. I enjoyed that.

Second, Vinnie, you probably haven't noticed, but these routes are all tested and true.

Not only have I not noticed, boss, but I don't even know what you're talking about.

I mean, Vinnie, that they are all carefully measured, so that they are neither too long nor too short. They're just right for you and me.

Why is that so important, boss?

That brings me to my third reason. These walks are good for us. If they were too long, we would get exhausted and tired. If they were too short, they wouldn't do us any good.

That's a good point, boss. Hopefully these daily walks will provide us with a better and longer life.

That they will, Vinnie, that they will.

Reflection:
1. What would it take to make my life complete?
2. Have I noticed any stirrings in my heart which need to be fulfilled?
3. In what way might a closer walk with Jesus fulfill those yearnings?

SIXTH SUNDAY OF EASTER

John 14:15-21

The disciples must have been very disappointed to learn that Jesus would be leaving them; certainly Jesus would have known that. Not wanting them to be lost without him, Jesus provided for them in his absence. He entrusted the care of his flock to the apostles and he sent the Holy Spirit to be with them. Through the action of the Holy Spirit, Jesus would continue to be present to them, guiding them and giving them courage. Jesus is with us even today. He is present in his Church and the gift of the Holy Spirit we have received from him. Jesus has gone back to the Father, but he will return and give us the gift of eternal life.

I'LL BE BACK

Are you all right, Vinnie? You look a little down in the mouth.

I'm feeling all right, boss. It's just that it's Tuesday, and you know what that means.

Yes, I know. It means that I'll be gone all day. But we did go out early this morning for our walk, so it's not all that bad.

I know, boss, and I really enjoyed our walk together. Maybe that's why I hate to see you go away. That means we won't have any more walks today.

No, Vinnie, we won't, but you know I'll be back, and there's always tomorrow.

I guess, I'll have to wait, won't I, boss? It just seems like a long way off. Sometimes I begin to wonder if you'll ever get home.

I haven't let you down yet, Vinnie, so you know you can count on me keeping my word.

Tell me, Vinnie, what do you do on these days when I'm away?

It's not a total disaster, boss. Fortunately, there are others here to keep me company.

That's right, Vinnie. You've got the whole office staff here and all the visitors who come to the office. It's not like you'll be left alone. I wouldn't let that happen.

No, we have a pretty good time together. Sometimes I even get a few extra treats, which I don't always tell you about; because you would tell me I'm getting too fat.

I think I suspected as much, Vinnie. I know you're not getting heavy on only what I feed you.

That's for sure, boss! So I guess I'll get by for another day.

I'm glad to hear you say that, Vinnie, because you know it's really important for me to have some time off.

I understand that, boss, and I wouldn't want you to give up your day away. You need a little time to recharge your batteries, just like the rest of us.

You're going to be all right then, Vinnie?

Oh my yes, boss. You may not be able to tell, but even when you're gone, I have many places to visit around the house that remind me of you. It's almost as if you yourself were here. In a way, you're gone, but you're not away.

Good boy, Vinnie. I'll be leaving now, but I'll be back.

Right, boss, and don't forget to bring me my treat.

Reflection:
1. Why was it better for us that Jesus left us?
2. How does Jesus continue to be present to us?
3. How often do I have recourse to the gifts of the Holy Spirit?

Now what if the children come to the door asking for cookies?   KENNETH PILCHER

ASCENSION OF THE LORD

Matthew 28:16-20

With the return of Jesus to the Father, the era of the Church begins. Left looking to the heavens, the disciples are told to return to Jerusalem. There, as they are gathered in prayer, they will experience the coming of the Holy Spirit and the Church will be born. Under the Spirit's influence, they will find that they are able to continue the works they have learned from their years spent with Jesus. They will preach and heal and sanctify in his name, and through them the ministry of Jesus will continue. Like the first disciples, we too are called to minister in our world today.

TAKE CHARGE

Don't tell me you're going away again, boss?
Yes, Vinnie, I have some calls to make and I'll probably be gone for a while.

That sounds like a long time to me, boss. What am I supposed to do while you're gone?

Well, Vinnie, you're on duty while I'm away.

What's that mean?

That means you take care of handling the parish while I'm gone. You're in charge.

It sounds like a pretty big responsibility, boss. Do you think I can handle it?

I'm sure you can, Vinnie. You've been here long enough to learn what needs to be done. I think you're ready to accept this responsibility.

I appreciate your trust, boss, but let me be sure about what I should do.

All right, Vinnie. Let's run through a few situations to see if you know what to do.

Good idea, boss. You tell me what might happen, and I'll tell you what I would do.

Okay, here goes. Let's say someone calls and asks for me. What would you tell them?

That's easy, boss, I'll just tell them you're away again, and you'll be back later.

That's good, but maybe you could drop the "again" part.

Now, what if the children come to the door asking for cookies?

That's an easy one, boss. I know exactly where the cookies are, so I just go to the door and give them some.

And don't forget, Vinnie, the cookies are for the children; not for you.

I can't promise you, boss, but I'll do the best I can. I'm sure there will be a few left for the children.

See there, Vinnie, I told you could do it. And you know how to greet any visitors who might come to the door. I've watched you do that over and over again.

Oh yes, I just run, get a toy, and let them know they are welcome by wagging my tail at them.

Good boy, Vinnie. You're going to be just fine, and I'll try to get back as soon as possible.

But, boss, what if I'm not sure what to do?

You know how to reach me. Just give me a call and I'll be there to help you.

Reflection:
1. In what ways does the Church continue the ministry of Jesus?
2. What ministries of the Church are in need of help today?
3. What can I do to be part of the Church's ministry?

He's away again and will be back later.
That's easy, boss, I'll just tell them you're away
again and will be back later

ABBY SOVACOOL

PENTECOST SUNDAY

John 7:37-39

John's gospel does not record a Pentecost event, unless we consider the appearance of Jesus on Easter Sunday evening as a kind of Pentecost. According to John, Jesus breathed on the apostles gathered in the upper room and said: "Receive the Holy Spirit." Together witwh the gift of the Holy Spirit, the apostles receive the power to forgive and retain sin. The Church has always seen this as the basis for the sacrament of reconciliation, by which the church continues the forgiving ministry of Jesus. The forgiveness of sins is not restricted to the sacrament of reconciliation. We who have the spirit of Jesus must become instruments of reconciliation, so that we might be a "forgiving Church."

ALL IS FORGIVEN

Did you notice that man paid absolutely no attention to you, Vinnie? You went up to say "hello", and he didn't even look at you.

Oh, it's all right, boss. Dogs know how to get over things like that.

I've noticed that about you, Vinnie. You are very quick to forgive people who offend you. I've often wondered how you manage to do that. We humans have trouble forgiving and forgetting. Why do you think that is?

I don't know about you people, boss, but I know we dogs have always remembered the lesson taught by Ur-dog.

Isn't Ur-dog the one who first learned to get along with humans and be their friend?

Correct-o, boss. Your memory isn't as bad as I thought it was.

I'll forgive that remark, Vinnie. Just tell me about Ur-dog.

Among us dogs the story is told of the time Ur-dog's boss told him he had to stay at home while the boss went on a hunting trip. As you might imagine, that was a very sad day for Ur-dog, since he loved nothing more than the hunt, but the boss was very firm and refused to give in.

So what happened then?

Ur-dog did as he was told. He stayed at home all day and moped. Eventually the boss returned and Ur-dog pretended that he didn't even notice. He let the boss know he was plenty upset.

But did he forgive the boss?

Be patient, boss, I'm getting to that. You see, Ur-dog discovered that being upset made him even sadder, so he went over and licked his boss's face and made up with him.

I guess that made everything all right, didn't it?

It did in a way, boss, but there's more to the story.

Tell me about it.

You see, Ur-dog learned many years later the reason the boss wouldn't let him go hunting that day.

What was it, Vinnie?

Ur-dog's boss knew that the animal he was hunting would attack Ur-dog and kill him. His boss was just looking out for Ur-dog. Ever since we dogs have been quick to forgive.

That's a beautiful story, Vinnie. I'm glad to know the spirit of Ur-dog still lives in you.

Reflection:
1. Why is it so hard to forgive?
2. Is forgiving without forgetting enough?
3. How can I forgive the people in my life I need to forgive?

ORDINARY TIME

SECOND SUNDAY IN ORDINARY TIME
John 1:29-34

John the Baptist came to herald the coming of Jesus. In the gospel today he not only calls attention to the presence of Jesus, but he also tells the people who Jesus is: the Lamb of God whose blood will cleanse them of their sins and restore them to everlasting life. Like John, each of us is called to reveal the presence of Christ among us. We do this first by allowing Christ's life to grow in us, so that our lives will shine forth with the light of Christ. We are also called to share in the evangelizing mission of the church, using whatever opportunities are available to us to point the way to Jesus for others. There are many who are searching for the fullness of life only Jesus can offer. You and I can help them by inviting them to "come and see."

ANSWERING THE DOOR

I'm going to need some help around the office today, Vinnie. It looks like you and I are the only ones here today.

I'm always happy to be of assistance, boss. What would you like me to do?

It would be helpful if you could help answer the door.

You know I'm not able to open the door, boss, but I can let you know when someone is here.

Yes, Vinnie, and you can also let me know who is at the door.

Gotcha, boss. I'll take care of that for you. You can go back to your office now.

Was that the doorbell, Vinnie?

It sure was, boss.

But I didn't hear you, Vinnie. I thought you were going to let me know who was here.

I'm doing that, boss. Can't you see me standing here wagging my tail?

I can see that, Vinnie, but I have trouble hearing your tail from my office.

Now wait just a doggone minute, boss, you told me to let you know who was at the door.

I can't do that and bark at the same time.

Why not, Vinnie, that doesn't sound too difficult?

No it isn't, boss, but if I bark, then the person at the door might think I'm being unfriendly, so I just wag my tail to let them know they're welcome.

I get it, Vinnie. So if I hear the doorbell and don't hear you, I know it is a friendly visitor at the door.

Right, boss.

Now, what are you barking for, Vinnie?

There's someone at the door.

I thought you were going to wag your tail.

I am, but these visitors need some instructions.

Who are they?

The children are here for cookies, so I'm telling them to go to the kitchen door.

Good. So if I hear you barking, then I know the children are here for cookies. But won't the barking frighten them?

Not this bark, boss. This is what's known as a friendly bark. The children know I'm not going to hurt them. I'm just letting you know they're here.

Keep it up, Vinnie, you're doing a fine job.

Whoa, Vinnie, that's a really loud bark. Is it the children again?

Not this time, boss. There's a fellow here who needs some assistance.

Isn't that loud bark going to frighten him away?

Not if he's alert, boss. He should be able to see that my tail is wagging, and that tells him I'm not going to hurt him.

But why such a loud bark, Vinnie?

Because I wanted to be sure you heard me, boss. This is really an important call, and I didn't want you to miss it.

Great, so now I know someone is at the door and looking for assistance.

That's right, boss. Now it's up to you to do something about it.

Reflection:

1. How can I increase the life of Christ within me this year?
2. What opportunities are available for me to invite others to find Christ?
3. For spiritual reading find a copy of Pope Paul VI's <u>Evangelii Nuntiandi</u>.

THIRD SUNDAY
IN ORDINARY TIME

Matthew 4: 12-17

In this Gospel text we find Jesus taking up a new residence. It seems the reason for his move was the arrest of John, which may have been a sign that Jesus was no longer safe in Nazareth. Whatever the reason, Jesus knew it was time for a change, and he adapted to the changing circumstances in which he found himself. This action by Jesus causes us to reflect on the many changes we experience: our life changes as we grow older: people in our lives move in and out, the world changes, the church changes. We can bemoan these changes, or we can learn to adapt to them. The choice is clear, and only one answer is appropriate.

THINGS CHANGE

You've been lying around all morning, Vinnie. Are you feeling all right?

I'm fine, boss, just a little tired.

I don't know why you should feel tired, Vinnie, you haven't done anything all day except help me open the church.

Are you forgetting, boss? You know I had a birthday this week, and I'm another year older.

Does that make so much difference, Vinnie?

You know how it is, boss. The years add up and gradually they take a toll. I'm not the young pup I used to be.

You're right about that, Vinnie. I guess we're all growing older, aren't we?

Yes, boss, but it's not the growing older that bothers me. It's just that I have to adapt to the changes that happen as I grow.

And what would those changes be?

Probably the most noticeable change is in my diet.

You would notice that, wouldn't you?

Well, that's pretty important, boss. I notice as I grow older and less active that I tend to gain weight if I eat the way I did when I was younger.

Are you trying to tell me that you don't eat as much as you used to?

I didn't say that, boss. But you will notice I've changed to a different dog food, one that is especially formulated for seniors and has less fat.

Yes, that's true. You have been eating a different food than when you were just a puppy.

You see, boss, by making that change I have been able to eat as much as always without the harmful side effect of gaining weight.

I'm not sure all would agree with that, Vinnie, but I admire your willingness to adapt.

That's the whole idea, boss. One must be willing to adapt to life's changes. It's not always easy, and it took a while for me to learn how to like that new food, but I've been able to do it, and now I'm living a healthier life.

That's a lesson we could all learn, isn't it Vinnie?

I think so, boss, but I don't like to tell people what to do. They have to learn for themselves how to notice life's changes and how to adapt.

Do you have any suggestions I can offer people?

Sure, boss. You can tell them to just watch me.

Reflection:
1. What are the most significant changes I have experienced in my life?
2. Which of these changes was the most difficult to accept?
3. How has the finger of God been made evident as a result of these changes?

CHRISTINA GOREY

FOURTH SUNDAY
IN ORDINARY TIME

Matthew 5: 1-12a

When the beatitudes speak of the poor or the poor in spirit, they do not imply that being destitute is a blessing—far from it. Poverty is a spiritual condition which leads us to put all our faith and trust in God. The person who does not rely on his or her own strength nor on worldly possessions realizes that God will provide all that is necessary to find happiness. Il Poverello, *St. Francis of Assisi owned nothing, but possessed everything. The next time you take a walk in the park, consider this: nothing in the park belongs to you: you do not own it, but it is yours to enjoy, and the joy you experience is no less real, because you do not own it. This is a lesson difficult to comprehend in a society of consumers, constantly bombarded with advertisements tempting one to believe in a need which does not exist.*

BLESSED ARE THE POOR

That wasn't very nice, Vinnie. Your barking scared those little sparrows right out of the bushes. Why did you do that?

I wasn't trying to scare them, boss, I just wanted to warn them to keep their eyes open. Sometimes they get a little too comfortable in these bushes and they need a wake up call.

And just what is it that they need to watch for, Vinnie? I should think they would be pretty safe hiding in our bushes.

You may think that, boss, but, as usual, you just don't get it.

Get what?

There's a hawk hanging out around here, boss, and sometimes he goes into the bushes where the sparrows live and then one of those little guys becomes the hawk's lunch.

I must congratulate you on being so observant, Vinnie. I confess, I hadn't noticed that.

That's part of my job around here, boss. Those little birds don't stand a chance against that hawk, but he wouldn't dare tangle with me.

I didn't know you were so concerned about the sparrows, Vinnie. Since when have you grown attached to them?

I can't say for sure, boss, but I think I like them because they are so small and helpless. They don't have the means to defend themselves, so they need me to help them. If they were bigger and stronger, I don't think I would care as much.

I like the sparrows also, Vinnie. As you know I make sure they have enough food to eat each day, but I don't know if I like them as much as you do. You are so protective of them.

As I said, boss, they need me, so I have a greater concern for them.

I suppose, Vinnie, if there were more you could do, you would do it.

Absolutely, boss. If I had my way, which I don't, I'd invite them into the house to live. It's so cold out here, I feel sorry for them.

Wouldn't that be something, Vinnie? We'd have sparrows flying all over the house. If they got hungry they could just fly over to your bowl and eat your food and drink your water.

Hold on, boss, I said I like them, but not that much!

Reflection:
1. Take a trip to a museum and experience the pleasure of seeing and not owning.
2. Try approaching your shopping center as a museum, where you can enjoy without buying and owning.
3. Look around you. How many of the things you see do you really need?

JACOB SINOPOLI

FIFTH SUNDAY
IN ORDINARY TIME

Matthew 5:13-16

God has gifted us with unique personalities and talents. When we use God's gifts in our discourse with the world, we are displaying in an oblique way the many facets of God's glory.

The poet Gerard M. Hopkins tells us that the world is "charged" with God's grandeur. Each of us can glorify the Lord by the good we do for others. We best show our gratitude to God by using well the gifts he has given us. Too often we fail to appreciate the source of our giftedness, claiming it as our own and growing prideful. Frequently remembering the source of all we have inspires us to pray in the words of the Psalmist: "Non nobis, Domine, non nobis, sed nomini tuo da gloriam: "Not to us, Lord, not to us, but to your name be the glory."

SHINING EXAMPLE

Boss, there are some strange things in my food dish.

Yes, Vinnie, those are some new treats I bought for you. I hope you like them.

Let me try them, boss. I'll let you know. Ummm, not bad, boss, not bad at all. I rather like them.

I'm not surprised at that, Vinnie. I haven't found anything yet you don't like.

Let's not get personal, boss, but tell me, what are these new treats supposed to do for me? Every time you find a new treat for me, there's a reason for it.

You're right about that, Vinnie. Actually these treats have a special purpose. They are supposed to relieve your drying skin and also keep your coat nice and shiny.

What's wrong with my coat, boss? I thought it was all right.

It's fine, Vinnie, and it serves its purpose by keeping you warm, but you'll have to admit that it's not as shiny as it once was.

I haven't looked in the mirror lately, but I wouldn't be surprised if what you say is true. After all I'm not the young pup I once was, and I suppose I'm starting to show my age.

Just a little, Vinnie, but these new treats will restore some of the luster you've lost, and you'll look as beautiful as ever. Not only will you look beautiful, but your fur will be soft and lustrous again.

I appreciate that, boss. I don't want to be vain or anything, but it's important for me to have a nice coat when you and I go walking.

Yes, people appreciate a dog that looks as good as you do. They keep telling me what a handsome dog you are, and I like hearing that.

That's part of it, boss. But there's an even more important reason.

What's that, Vinnie?

You see, boss, some people we meet on the street are pretty stressed out. Some of them are lonely and don't have anybody who really cares about them. These are the people who often ask you if it's all right to pet me. If my fur stays soft and fluffy, they'll keep doing that.

That's true, Vinnie. It's interesting isn't it, how people seem to relax just by running their fingers through your hair?

I know, boss. I can't help it. I just seem to attract people to myself.

You do, Vinnie, but don't forget where that shiny coat is coming from. Without these treats, you might not be so irresistible.

There's no way I'm going to forget that, boss. I'm sure you will continue to remind me about it. Now what do you say you and I go for a walk?

Reflection:
1. What talents and gifts has God given to me?
2. Am I aware of the source of all I have and thank God?
3. Am I using my God given gifts to benefit others?

SIXTH SUNDAY
IN ORDINARY TIME

Matthew 5:17-37

We know that Jesus expects a higher code of behavior from his disciples. It is not enough that we refrain from killing; we must try to practice kindness and not grow angry. If Jesus moves beyond the prescriptions of the Old Law and asks his followers to do the same, it is not because we are any better than our ancestors in the faith. It is because of the closer relationship we have with God in Christ. Jesus revealed a God who is first and foremost a loving father, who sent his son to be our brother. Because of this bond of love, we must respond to God as a lover to his or her beloved.

NOBLESSE OBLIGE

What are you looking at, Vinnie?

I was watching that dog in our yard and wishing I could join him.

But, Vinnie, that dog is running free. Look he has no collar, and it looks as if he hasn't had a bath in months

That's just it, boss. You know what I think of baths, and to think that I could just get up and go anytime I wished, with no collar and no leash, that just seems too good to be true.

I think you would find it's not the way you think it would be. You might be free to do whatever you wanted, but if I know you, I think you might get tired to having to go out and find your own food each day.

You've got a point there, boss.

Not only that, Vinnie, but you're not like all the other dogs out there.

I'm not? What's so different about me?

Well, you're a dog all right, and in some respects you're no better or worse than other dogs, but your present position sets you apart as a unique and special dog, and that brings with it the need for you to act in an appropriate way.

That all sounds rather pretentious, boss. What exactly are you talking about?

For one thing, you're a church dog and that brings with it certain responsibilities.

Excuse my asking, boss, but just what are you referring to?

You have to behave better than other dogs. You can't go chasing after people who come here to visit, and you can't start barking at them as if they weren't welcome here.

Other dogs do that, boss?

Some of them do, especially those who don't have a home like you do.

I suppose you're right, boss. I never thought of that.

And also, Vinnie, you have me.

What's that got to do with it, boss?

Well, you and I have a special relationship. I provide a home and food for you, and you agree to stay here and not go running all over town.

You've got that partly right, boss, but you're really missing the most important thing.

I am?

Sure. I behave the way I do because I love you and you love me. I wouldn't do anything to offend you.

I appreciate that, Vinnie, and that's why you and I are such good friends.

Reflection:

1. How can I grow in my appreciation of God's love for me?
2. Do I observe God's commandments out of fear?
3. How would my behavior change if I acted out of love rather than fear?

SEVENTH SUNDAY
IN ORDINARY TIME

Matthew 5:38-48

The gospel for today is one of the most beautiful and most challenging in all the scriptures. Loving those who insult us, not insisting on our rights, accepting injustices in silence and loving our enemy are practices we have trouble understanding and even more trouble doing. Once again, Jesus challenges us to rise above our human nature to become more like God in loving one another. God sees beyond appearances to the goodness in the hearts of each one of us. Regardless of who we are, what we do, or what we have; God loves us and calls us to be our best self.

A TRUE GENTLEMAN

Slow down, boss, I think I see someone I know up ahead.

You should know him, Vinnie. Isn't he the man that always has a treat for you when he sees you?

That's the one, boss, so let's just slow down. He probably wants to greet me and pat me on the head a little. I guess it makes him feel better.

I'm sure it does, Vinnie, and that's why he always has a treat ready for you. He wants to be sure that you will stop to greet him.

He's a smart man, boss. He knows the way to win a dog's affection.

If you're finished eating now, Vinnie, maybe we can continue our walk.

Right, boss. Who knows? We might run into some other nice people.

I think I see someone ahead of us now, Vinnie. Do you recognize him?

I can't say that I do, boss. Let's keep walking. Maybe I'll recognize him when we get closer.

I don't know about this man, Vinnie. I've never seen him before.

Neither have I, boss, and from the way he looks, I doubt very much that he has any treats in his pocket for me.

I agree with you, Vinnie. That poor man looks like any treats he may have he needs for himself. I'll wager he's been wearing those clothes for several weeks, and he really needs a bath and a shave.

You're right, boss, but he seems to want to talk with us.

My, what a nice dog! Can I pet him?

Sure, he loves it when people pet him.

I used to have a dog. My dog wasn't as handsome as yours, but I loved him and I sure do miss him.

All dogs are good dogs, aren't they? It doesn't matter what they look like. You love them and you know they love you.

What's your dog's name?

He's a church dog, and his name is Vinnie.

You're a nice dog, Vinnie, and it's a pleasure to meet you.

Thank you, sir; it's a pleasure to meet you also. I wish I had a treat to offer you, but I'm all out.

That's no problem, Vinnie. Thank you for thinking of me. Not many people are as gentle with me as you are.

I'm sorry to hear that. If they got to know you better, they would find that you are a gentle man, like me. Have a nice day.

I will now, Vinnie. Thank you.

Reflection:

1. How do I relate to people who seem not to like me?
2. Do I seem to love only the people I like?
3. Have you ever found that people you don't like at first, turn out to be good friends after you get to know them?

EIGHTH SUNDAY
IN ORDINARY TIME

Matthew 6:24-34

I know very little German, but the one Sunday I attended Mass in Austria there was one word the priest repeated several times. The word was "angst." I don't know what he said about it, but I know he was talking about a problem common to us all— "anxiety." Jesus tells us today that our anxiety is caused by our failure to make the proper choice in what guides our life. If our goal in life is to serve and obtain the kingdom of heaven, then God, our loving Father, will take care of the other concerns we have: food and clothing and shelter. If we find ourselves growing anxious over the needs of our lives, perhaps we need to look more deeply to find if we are making these needs more important than they should be.

I'LL TAKE CARE OF IT

You seem awfully nervous today, Vinnie.
I'm not nervous, boss, I'm just checking.

That's the fifth time this morning you've been over to look at your empty food bowl. What are you looking for?

What do you think I'm looking for boss? I'm looking for food.

But you already ate your food.

I know, boss, but I was wondering if there might be more.

Don't worry, Vinnie. I'll refill it in the morning.

Yeah, right, boss.

Where are you going now, Vinnie?

I'm going over to the door by the courtyard.

What are going there for?

I need to go out.

I suppose you expect me to come with you to open the door.

Well, you know I can't open it by myself, so if I'm going to get out, I guess you'll have to open the door, won't you?

You seem to take a lot for granted, Vinnie. What if I weren't here, what would you do then?

I never gave it thought, boss. You're always there when I need you.

What day is it today, boss?

It's Sunday, why do you ask?

Why do I ask? For heaven's sake, boss, let's get going.

Where are we going?

To church. It's Sunday isn't it? It's time for us to get over to church. They're going to be waiting for me.

Just be patient, Vinnie, it's much too early. There isn't anybody in church yet. You'll have to wait a while.

Okay, boss.

Now what, Vinnie?

It's been a while, boss. Let's get over to the church.

It's still a bit early, Vinnie. Just wait a few more minutes. Besides, why are you so anxious to get to the church today? You never seem so anxious on other days.

But today is Sunday, boss, and there are people there with treats for me. I don't want to miss them.

I thought it would be something like that, but don't worry, Vinnie, I'll get you there in time.

I know you will, boss, you always do.

Try to remember that, Vinnie, and you won't be so anxious.

Reflection:
1. What do I find myself worrying about?
2. Would a greater trust in God's kindness and mercy help resolve my fears?
3. Am I sufficiently grateful for the care God has always provided?

NINTH SUNDAY
IN ORDINARY TIME

Matthew 7:21-27

GET REAL

So often we, as Christians, are challenged to explain our actions of the past, such as the Inquisition or, more recently, the clergy sexual abuses. Such sins call into question the value of religion in general, and the Catholic expression of Christianity in particular. Undoubtedly, we are embarrassed by these faults and pray they may never happen again. If nothing else, the recognition of these errors should prompt each of us to strive even more diligently to put into practice the truths we profess.

Is there something wrong with that man, boss? He seems to be a little upset?

There's nothing wrong with him, Vinnie, I think he's a little worried about you.

That's strange, boss. Why should he be worried about me? He doesn't even know me.

That's just the point, Vinnie. He doesn't know how kind and gentle you are, so he has to worry about you.

Do you mean to say he's worried about me just because I'm a dog? What's the man got against dogs?

It could be that he's been bitten by a dog in the past and now he doesn't trust any dogs. Or maybe he's just afraid of large dogs like you, because large dogs can be especially dangerous.

I guess I can understand that, boss, but it doesn't seem right to judge a dog by its size. He ought to get to know me a little better before he starts getting all nervous about me.

Let me talk to him, Vinnie. Maybe we can help him.

Good morning. It's a beautiful morning for a walk isn't it?

Does that dog bite?

(Did I hear him right, boss? Did he ask if I bite? What's wrong with him, of course I bite! All dogs bite. Doesn't he know that?)

Hold on a minute, Vinnie, just calm down.

No, this dog won't bite. He's very gentle.

(Let's not push that gentle thing too far, boss. I can still bite you know.)

I know that, Vinnie, but we need to play that idea down right now.

Wait, isn't that the St. Vincent dog?

Yes, it is. His name is Vinnie.

Oh, I know him. Good morning, Vinnie.

Good morning, my man. I'm glad you finally recognized me. I don't like to frighten people. I prefer they pet me and offer me a treat.

I'm sorry, but I didn't recognize you at first. If I had known you were from St. Vincent, I wouldn't have been afraid.

Why do you say that?

Because you're a church dog, and church dogs don't bite. They learn to practice what they preach.

Did you hear that, boss? Just like I've been telling you, there's more to being a church dog than just living there. You've got to talk the talk and walk the walk.

Reflection:
1. What teachings of Jesus are difficult for me to practice?
2. What do I find offensive in the policies of my church?
3. What can I do to help change those policies?

Hey boss look!   AARIS DOWLING

TENTH SUNDAY
IN ORDINARY TIME

Matthew 9:9-13

Things haven't changed much since the time of Jesus. We are still very conscious of whom we invite to dine with us, and the places we choose to eat out at are chosen with a view to the kind of people we will find there. While we may find it hard to overcome this form of class consciousness, Jesus teaches us that it has no place in his church. Jesus may have scandalized the people of his time, but he made it very clear that everybody is welcome at his table, and he expects the same behavior among his followers. We may want to avoid eating at the "greasy spoon" restaurant in town, but it should be because of the food and not the people who eat there.

COME TO THE TABLE

It's such a nice day, Vinnie, how about you and I taking a ride?

Sounds like a good idea to me, boss. Where would you like to go?

I thought we might go down to Amish country and enjoy the scenery.

It's all right with me, boss, but what's an "Amish?"

TheAmish are a sect of the Mennonite religion, and their name comes from their founder, Jacob Amman. They are quite strict and the way they live is different from ours.

You've got my interest, boss. Let's take a look see.

I'm beginning to understand why you wanted to come here, boss. This is really beautiful country. It reminds me of the rolling hills of Switzerland.

What are you talking about? You've never been in Switzerland.

I know, but I've seen them on television. Wow! Look over there, boss. Look at all those cows and sheep. This is getting more interesting all the time.

I knew you would enjoy seeing the other animals, Vinnie, but try to behave yourself and not get too excited about them.

You know me, boss, the model of etiquette and decorum.

Whoa, boss! What was that that just shot by us?

That was an Amish buggy being pulled by a horse. That's how the Amish get around. They don't have cars, so they use their horses to pull their buggies around.

Hmm, very interesting, boss. I'll keep my eyes open.

I think I'll pull in here for a while, Vinnie. You wait in the car for me, while I get a bite to eat.

Okay, boss, but don't be long. Oops, hold on, boss.

What is it, Vinnie?

This parking lot. Haven't you noticed?

Noticed what?

It's one of those buggies, and there's a horse attached to it. Roll down the window so I can tell them to go to their own parking lot. That horse doesn't have any business parking here.

Now just settle down, Vinnie, before you have a heart attack. That horse has as much right to be here as you do, so just get used to it.

I wonder about you, sometimes, boss. You sure pick some unusual people to eat with.

While I'm gone, you can talk with that horse. Maybe you'll learn something.

Yeah, right, boss. Enjoy your lunch. I'll keep an eye on this horse.

Reflection:

1. Are there certain people in church I find hard to get along with?
2. Is our parish open to accepting outsiders and people of different races and cultures?
3. What could our parish do to become more welcoming to others?

Whoa, boss! What was that that just shot by us?

TORY KOVALCHICK

ELEVENTH SUNDAY
IN ORDINARY TIME

Matthew 9:36-10:8

I don't think Jesus ever intended the work of the church to be confined only to those who are the "professionals": priests, ministers, religious. By baptism, all are brought into the mission of spreading the "good news", each in his or her own way. Parents hand on the faith to their children, both by word and example and church members get involved in many ministries which are necessary for the church to be effective. They help teach in our schools of religion; they visit the sick in our hospitals and nursing homes; they assist in procuring the funds necessary for the church to exist. There are many ministries available for those who are willing to put their talents to use for the work of sharing the gospel with others.

MAY I HELP YOU?

You seem very busy, Vinnie. What are you working on?

I was just putting together a list of the ways I might be able to help you around here. You seem to be so busy all the time, I thought maybe I could help.

Good idea, Vinnie. Do you mind if I take a look at your list?

Sure thing, boss, see what you think.

Let's see: helping to prepare lunch; helping to clean the dishes; helping with the grocery shopping. I don't know about this list, Vinnie, it seems to have a common theme running through it.

I knew that, boss, but I thought it might escape your attention.

Not likely, Vinnie, although I must admit these are all things you would be good at.

What would your list look like, boss? Are there any ways in which you think I might be able to help?

Let's think about that, Vinnie. I'm sure there are some things you can do which would be of more assistance than the ones you thought of.

I'm open to any suggestions, boss.

There's one thing you do very well, Vinnie, in addition to eating.

What's that, boss?

You are very good at cheering up people. You always bring a smile to their faces, and that's a good thing.

You're right about that, boss. How can we put that asset to good use?

Perhaps you could go to school with me and help me teach the children. The children are always glad to see you.

True enough, boss, but that may not necessarily help you. Sometimes the children pay more attention to me than to you.

You've got a point there, Vinnie. Let's think again.

I've got it, boss; I could go to the nursing home with you to visit the people who live there.

That's a great idea, Vinnie. You'd be perfect at that. Sometimes people in nursing homes get a little depressed and they need someone like you to lift their spirits.

Sure, boss. I'll bet a lot of them once had a dog like me, and I could help them remember. Who knows? They may even have few treats left.

Do I notice a familiar theme creeping in here, Vinnie?

No need to be concerned, boss. I just thought I'd mention it.

Reflection:
1. What talents do I have to offer the church?
2. What opportunities for ministry are available at my church?
3. What would I have to do to get involved?

TWELFTH SUNDAY IN ORDINARY TIME

Matthew 10:26-33

In apostolic times it required real courage to profess one's faith in Christ. Being a Christian could lead to being expelled from the synagogue, losing one's property and position, and in times of persecution it meant even death. In a Christian society like our own, these threats no longer exist. The difficulty in being a Christian today is to rise above the easy way and embrace the teachings of Christ in a more radical way. Often this leads to misunderstanding and exclusion from a society which has reduced the practice of Christianity to a religion which makes few demands and promises many worldly rewards. Courage to be a Christian is still important, even if the threats have changed. Believing that God will protect us gives us the courage we need.

COURAGE UNDER FIRE

Yikes, boss! What is that?

I'm not sure, Vinnie. I think it might be the sound coming from the program I'm watching on television.

Well, if it is, turn it off. That sound is ear piercing. It sounds like the wailing of a banshee, and to tell you the truth, I'm scared.

All right, Vinnie, I'll turn off the television.

Sorry, boss, that didn't do any good. I can still hear it.

So can I, Vinnie. Let's look around and see where it's coming from.

Out here, boss, it's coming from out here in the hallway.

So it is, Vinnie, and it's just what I suspected. It's the fire alarm.

The fire alarm! Come on, boss, let's get out of here before the house falls down on us.

Let's not lose our cool, Vinnie. After all, it may be only a false alarm.

I'll tell you one thing, boss. If this house is on fire, we're going to lose our cool real fast. Maybe we should just step outside for a few minutes and watch from out there.

I don't think that will be necessary, Vinnie. Let's just walk around the house and we'll see if we can smell any smoke.

Walk around the house until we smell smoke and then we'll know there's a fire. That's a really dumb idea, boss. Did it ever enter your head that we might call the fire department and then high tail it out of here?

Oh, come on, Vinnie, where's your sense of adventure?

I think that alarm deadened it a bit, but if you're going to smell around the house, I suppose I'd better come with you. You're going to need my smeller.

Nothing on the first floor, Vinnie, everything seems pretty normal.

I don't smell anything either, boss. Maybe we ought to leave the house now.

Not yet, Vinnie, we still have to check out the basement and the second and third floors.

Oh, great, boss, nothing like being down in the basement when fire strikes. You know, being a church dog can test one's courage.

But you're doing fine, Vinnie. Just stay by me and you'll be all right.

Don't worry, boss, I'm right at your side.

Reflection:
1. Who are some of the courageous Christians of our times?
2. Has our society, which is professedly religious, softened the Christian gospel?
3. What demands of Christ are difficult to follow today?

THIRTEENTH SUNDAY
IN ORDINARY TIME

Matthew 10:37-42

"Love me, love my dog." I'm not sure what that is supposed to mean, but for me it has always meant that when you show appreciation for my dog, I also consider it a compliment. I guess that's why I thank people when they remark how beautiful a dog Vinnie is. With this experience, I can appreciate what Jesus meant when he said that doing something for one of his "little ones" was like doing it for him. There are many "little ones" in our world on whom we might lavish our attention: the unborn and the born, the lonely poor and the lonely rich, the sick in body, mind and soul. Giving a cup of cold water to such as these will always be appreciated by the Lord.

THANKS FOR THE BISCUIT

Do you know that woman, boss?

I can't say that I do, Vinnie. Why do you ask?

Because she went running back into her house, as if she were afraid of something or someone.

You don't think she was afraid of you, do you Vinnie?

Why should she be afraid of me, boss? She's never seen me before.

That's just it, Vinnie. Sometimes people are afraid of dogs, especially large dogs like you.

Isn't that silly, boss? If she really knew me, she would know how gentle I am. I wouldn't hurt a flea.

You wouldn't?

Well, maybe a flea, if it got under my skin.

Look again, Vinnie. She's running out of her house now.

She sure is, boss, and she's running right toward us. Now it's my turn to be a little frightened.

Don't worry, Vinnie, I don't think she means to harm you.

What makes you say that, boss? Sometimes people like to chase us dogs away with a stick or something like that.

I don't think that's the case, Vinnie. The woman is carrying something, but it's not a stick. I'm not sure what it is.

Don't run away, doggie, I have something for you.

Doggie! Who's she calling doggie? Doesn't she know who I am?

Calm down, Vinnie. I think she wants to hand you a treat.

Why didn't you say so, boss? Why thank you, ma'am. That's a fine biscuit. You wouldn't have any more would you?

Now don't get greedy, Vinnie. It was nice of the lady to go to all that trouble to get you a biscuit.

You're right, boss. I wonder why she would do that?

I think I might know the answer to that, Vinnie. Look at those children coming down the street. Do you recognize any of them?

Of course, boss. Those are the children who come to our house for cookies. What's that got to do with it?

The lady who gave you the biscuit is their mother and she wanted to give you something for being nice to her children.

Reflection:

1. Have you known satisfaction in seeing someone being nice to your loved ones?

2. Helping those in need is another way of loving God. Do I show God love in this way?

3. Is it hard for me to remember that all people are God's children?

FOURTEENTH SUNDAY
IN ORDINARY TIME

Matthew 11:25-30

Among all the virtues, Jesus chooses to identify humility as the one he associates with himself. As important as humility is, we find it difficult to strike a balance between genuine humility and healthy self- respect. At what point does self- respect and appreciation for the gifts we have received become pride? True humility lies not in denigrating ourselves, but in recognizing our giftedness, not as something we have earned, but as something God has granted us. We should thank God, for "we are wonderfully made," and use our various gifts for the greater honor of God and for the benefits we can give to others through our giftedness.

HUMILITY

Who were you talking with, boss?

I was on the phone with someone who wants us to come and sign your book.

Are we going, boss?

I suppose we should, after all everybody is anxious to meet you. They've never known a dog who is also a famous author.

I don't know about that "famous" part, boss, but I am somewhat special, wouldn't you say?

No question about it, Vinnie. You're one of the best known dogs around town. I sometimes think more people know your name than they do mine.

Yes, I've noticed that also, boss. Sometimes I'm embarrassed when people want to talk to me and don't say anything to you.

That's all right, Vinnie, I'm used to it.

I think about that often, boss. I try to figure out what makes me so attractive.

Is that so? And what answers have you come up with?

There's no getting around it, boss, a lot has to do with my good looks.

No kidding, is that what you think?

Well, you have to admit, boss, the women all go crazy over me, and I really can't blame them. As one of them put it, I'm a handsome dog.

What about the men, Vinnie? What is it that makes them like you so much?

That's hard to say, boss. I think it has to do with their good taste in dogs.

Good taste in dogs, eh?

Yes, men appreciate a dog who is strong and healthy looking, a dog that would make a good hunting companion or watchdog, and I've got all of that.

If nothing, else, Vinnie, I would have to say you have a very positive self-image. To think, on top of all of that, you are a published author. I'm surprised we haven't heard from Oprah or Rachel yet.

I'm a little surprised myself, boss. I mean to talk to my agent about that.

Your agent—you've got an agent?

I'm working on it.

While you're working on it, why don't we go for our walk?

Good idea, boss, and while we're out, do you think we could stop at the store for a pair of sunglasses?

Reflection:
1. What gifts has God given me?
2. How am I using these gifts in a fruitful way?
3. Do I sometimes take credit for the gifts I possess?

FIFTEENTH SUNDAY
IN ORDINARY TIME

Matthew 13:1-23

*The parable of the sower is understood by most scrip-
ture scholars to have gone through a transition from
the original intent of Jesus to an interpretation meant
for those who had heard the word and reacted to it in
various ways. The original intent of the parable was
to emphasize the effectiveness of God's word which
comes down from heaven and does not return there
until it has watered the earth. God's word is powerful
and effective and it will always produce a change in
our hearts. The later interpretation, focusing as it does
on the types of soil into which the seed falls, places the
emphasis on the hearers of the word. As such, we must
allow the word to sink into our hearts, turning it over
in our minds, allowing it to take root in our lives.*

REAP WHAT YOU SOW

What are you doing out there, Vinnie?

I'm checking on the garden, boss. It seems the
tomato plants are doing very well. It won't be long

before we have some nice homegrown tomatoes to feast on.

I hope you're right, Vinnie. There's nothing like having your own tomatoes.

I couldn't agree with you more, boss. Now if you'll excuse me, I've got some work to do.

All right, Vinnie, I'll see you later.

Are you still out here, Vinnie? What are you doing now?

I'm digging some holes, boss.

So I see. What are you going to do with all those holes?

I've got some planting to do. The tomatoes have done so well, I figured this must be good soil for growing things, so I'm going to grow a few things for myself.

It's a little late for growing, Vinnie, but what exactly did you have in mind?

Bones.

Bones? What do you mean bones?

I'm going to plant a few bones out here. Just imagine, if my bones do as well as your tomatoes, I'll have enough bones to last me all winter. As you said, there's nothing to compare with homegrown bones.

But, Vinnie, you can't grow bones like you grow tomatoes.

Why not, boss. This is good soil, isn't it?

Yes, of course it is, Vinnie, but bones don't grow in the ground the way tomatoes do

They don't?

No, bones come from animals, and as you know, animals are born, not grown.

Do you mean to tell me that I've wasted all these good bones for nothing?

I'm afraid so, Vinnie. You might be able to dig them up and use them later, but they sure aren't going to grow any more bones.

I guess I've learned something, boss. I thought this soil was good enough to grow just about anything. Now you're telling me it won't grow bones. That sure is a disappointment.

Don't feel too bad, Vinnie, you can still chew on these bones.

Right, boss, and now I know good soil needs good seeds.

Reflection:
1. Is daily reading of the Bible part of my prayer?
2. What parts of the Bible do I find most helpful?
3. How is my life changed by reflecting on God's word?

SIXTEENTH SUNDAY IN ORDINARY TIME

Matthew 13:24-30

The parable of the weeds growing along side the wheat is as relevant today as it ever was. In every society there will be those who cause us distress and suffering. Some times it's a pesky neighbor. For those living in urban areas, it may be the criminal element that threatens our safety. Unfortunately, there are people who are not always thinking of others rather than themselves. It's not only civic society that has weeds growing alongside the wheat, but the same applies to our churches. There are those who cause suffering for others and those who demand we conform to their way. It has been and always will be a problem we cannot escape. We can only be patient and perhaps pray for them to change.

PLAYMATES

Where are we going for our walk today, boss?

I thought we might go back to the dog park so you could run and play with some other dogs. You seemed to enjoy it the last time we were there.

I sure did, boss, but I'm not so sure I want to go back there.

Really? I'm surprised to hear you say that, Vinnie. Why wouldn't you want to go back again?

Most of the dogs were very nice, boss, and they were fun to play with, but to tell you the truth, there were some dogs there I didn't particularly care for.

I hadn't noticed that, Vinnie. Which dogs are you referring to?

I'm not surprised you didn't notice, boss. After all, you don't understand the way we dogs do. But some of those dogs were a royal pain.

Tell me about it, Vinnie. What was it that bothered you?

To begin with, boss, some of those little dogs got under my skin.

Why was that, Vinnie?

It was the way they ran around chasing all the larger dogs and yapping utter nonsense. I mean, there was no need for them to carry on like that, they could have gone about their business like the rest of us. We didn't need to listen to all that chatter.

I can understand how that might be a problem, Vinnie. So what else bothered you?

Just between you and me, boss, it seemed some of those dogs thought they were a cut above the rest of us.

Some of those dogs have a real pedigree, Vinnie. They're not the same as those of you who don't have papers.

I know that, boss, but I got the impression that they didn't care to play with those of us who, as you say, "don't have papers."

I'm sorry to hear these things, Vinnie, maybe we should just go walking by ourselves today.

Oh no, boss, I didn't mean that. Let's go to the dog park. It will be a nice change.

But what about those dogs you don't like?

I'll just have to put up with them, boss. Fortunately, there are enough good dogs to make up for them.

Reflection:
1. Who are the people that bother me?
2. How can I learn to deal with these people?
3. Who or what are some of the weeds growing in our church?

SEVENTEENTH SUNDAY
IN ORDINARY TIME

Matthew13:44-52

We go through life searching for those things that will bring us happiness and fulfillment. More often than not what we are looking for finds us. Meaningful relationships may be the result of a chance meeting, interesting hobbies may develop from hearing a piece of music or responding to an invitation we received in the mail. When these things happen, we may think we have found what we were looking for—or did they find us? In our search for God, are we the ones searching, or is God searching for us? Perhaps our search is only an opening to the possibility of God finding us.

FINDERS KEEPERS

What are you doing in there, boss? You seem awfully busy.

No, it's not that I'm busy, Vinnie, I'm just trying to find a book.

If you don't mind my saying so, boss, don't you think you would have better luck finding a book in your bookshelf than in a computer?

What I mean, Vinnie, is that I'm trying to find where I can buy this particular book. I'm not looking for the book itself.

Why didn't you say so, boss? Let me know when you find it. Maybe you and I can go to the store to get it.

Uh-oh, Vinnie, it looks like we won't be going to any store. It says here that the book I'm looking for is out of print.

I'm sorry to hear that, boss. I was hoping we could stop at the pet store while we were out shopping. There are a few items there I need.

I can't imagine that there is anything you need, Vinnie, but come on, let's go out anyway. I'm getting a little tired on sitting in this office. It might help to get out and clear our heads.

My head's already pretty clear, boss, but I'll be happy to go out and help you clear yours.

Thanks, Vinnie, and maybe we can stop at that pet store while we're out.

Sounds like a plan, boss, let's go.

Look, boss, there's a bookstore next to the pet store and it looks like they're having a sidewalk sale.

It sure does, Vinnie, it's a clearance sale, and they want to get rid of some of the books they can't sell.

I'm in no hurry, boss, so if you want to stop and take a look at what they have, it's all right with me. Tell me the name of that book you were looking for, I'll help you look for it.

Good idea, Vinnie. It's a long shot, but it's worth a quick look.

Over here, boss, I think I may have found it.

Really? Let me see. By golly, Vinnie, you're right! Imagine that, we came to find a treat for you, and we found the book they said was out of print.

That really is a coincidence, boss. That book must feel the way I did when you found me. The book thought nobody cared about it, and now it has found an owner. You found the book and the book has found you. That's great!

Reflection:
1. Think back to some life changing event in your life.
2. Recall how it came about.
3. Did you make it happen, or was just happenstance — an act of God?

Why are you up here, Vinnie?
Because I was feeling blue. You know I don't like it
when you're away!

BRIAN TAVOLIER

EIGHTEENTH SUNDAY
IN ORDINARY TIME

Matthew 14:13-21

Hearing of the death of John the Baptist, Jesus retired to the other side of the lake to be alone. It wasn't long before people followed him there, and he fed and healed them. Perhaps Jesus is teaching his disciples that the Eucharistic gathering is his gift to us to help us in our times of hurt and mourning. It is normal for us to want to retire and not face others when we are suffering from grief and loss. Complete comfort will not be found in solitude, although we may need a period of solitude. In the end, we need the comfort that comes from gathering once again with family and friends. This is the reason we gather for a meal following a funeral. It is an opportunity to reconnect and move on with our lives. The Eucharist provides an opportunity to gather with our church family, where we will find the help we are looking for.

NOT GOOD TO BE ALONE

Yoo-hoo, Vinnie, I'm home. I wonder where Vinnie is; maybe he's out in the courtyard. No, he's not there. This is strange, Vinnie always runs to greet me when I come in from my day away. I think it has something to do with the treat I always bring him. I'll check the other rooms. I hope there isn't anything wrong. Vinnie, Vinnie, I'm home!

Oh well, maybe he's gone home with somebody. I'm sure he'll be back. I'll go up and change into something more comfortable.

Ah, there you are, Vinnie. What are you doing up on the third floor and where have you been? I looked all over for you.

Sorry, boss, I didn't hear you come in. I was upstairs.

That's a little unusual for you, isn't it, Vinnie? You're usually the first one to greet me when I come home.

Yes, I know, boss, but I was just feeling a little lonely and blue. You know I don't like it when you go away.

I know that, Vinnie, but why did you go upstairs to wait for me?

I just felt I needed to get away for awhile, boss. Sometimes when I feel down in the dumps, I like to get away from everyone and just be by myself.

Does that make you feel any better, Vinnie?

Not really, boss, it doesn't seem to help at all. Come to think of it, I probably feel worse than ever. I'm just one of those dogs that like to be around people, and when everyone is gone, it's really hard for me.

Well, let's go downstairs, Vinnie. I have a treat for you.

Great, boss! I'm feeling better already. What did you bring me?

One of your favorites, a pig ear.

You made short work of that, Vinnie. Are you feeling better now?

Much better, boss.

It's amazing what a pig ear can do to lift your spirits, Vinnie.

Yes, boss, but it's not only the pig ear. I appreciate that, don't get me wrong, but it's really your being here and my not being alone that helps the most.

I'm glad to hear you say that, Vinnie. Now we're getting back to normal.

Just about, boss, but I'm looking forward to tomorrow, when the whole gang is here and we can eat together.

Reflection:
1. Have I known times when I want to be alone?
2. When is it good and necessary to be alone?
3. How does the company of others help life my spirits?

I bet Vinnie will be so happy to see me!
What are you doing up on the third floor?

LIA GIFFELS

NINETEENTH SUNDAY
IN ORDINARY TIME

Matthew 14: 22-33

We cannot hope to encounter only calm seas in our journey on earth. There will be storms and rough seas. When our lives take a turn for the worse, we begin to worry and wonder about how to get through. Tough times, like stormy weather will pass, but until they do we must continue on, sometimes questioning how we will handle the present and uncertain of what lies in our future. Sometimes we just travel on in the midst of uncertainty, trusting that the Lord is at our side and that he will lead us safely home.

STORMY SEAS

Are we going for our walk today, boss?

I don't know, Vinnie, the weather doesn't look very good to me.

That never stopped us before, boss. Don't tell me you're going to let a little rain stop you?

It's not just the rain, Vinnie. They're predicting strong winds and thunderstorms. It could be pretty rough out there today.

Don't worry about it, boss. Just get my raincoat out and I'm ready to go.

If you say so, Vinnie. Let me get my raincoat and we'll be on our way.

It's not so bad out here, is it, boss? The wind is a little strong, but to tell you the truth, it feels good.

Yes it does, Vinnie, but those dark clouds in the west look a bit threatening, don't you think?

Oh! I hadn't noticed them, boss, but you are right, they are really dark. Do you think we should turn around?

It's too late now, Vinnie. We're as far from home as we're going to be, so turning around won't do any good. We may as well just keep on walking and hope for the best.

Right, boss, maybe we can outrun the storm.

Did you feel that, boss?

Did I feel what, Vinnie?

I think I felt a drop of rain land on my forehead. Uh-oh, here it comes. I think we're in for it, boss. This is going to be a lollapalooza.

What did you say, Vinnie, I can hardly hear you with this wind?

Don't look now, boss, but this rain is coming down in sheets. A lot of good this raincoat is going to be. Whose idea was it to come out in this weather?

If I'm not mistaken, you're the one who said we shouldn't let a little rain stop us.

Are you sure we're going in the right direction, boss? I can't even see in all this rain.

I'm certain of that, Vinnie. Don't worry. I'm not going to stay out in this any longer than necessary. I should have followed my instincts and waited a while.

Let's not debate that issue right now, boss. Let's just keep moving. Wow! Look at that lightning. You're not worried are you, boss?

Not really, are you?

Not at all, boss. You're here, and I'm sure you'll get us home.

Reflection:
1. Reflect back on some of the storms you have encountered in life.
2. What allowed you to get through?
3. Is your faith stronger today because of those times and the Lord's presence?

TWENTIETH SUNDAY
IN ORDINARY TIME

Matthew 16:13-20

As Jesus travelled in gentile lands, he encountered a woman who must have heard of the wonderful works he had done among his own people. Asking help for her daughter, she is rebuffed by Jesus, since she is not Jewish. The woman persists, however, humbly responding that even dogs eat the crumbs from their master's table. Impressed by her faith, Jesus grants her request. When our prayers go unanswered, we must continue to believe in God's love and continue seeking until we receive an answer. The answer is not always the one we are looking for, but if we persist, God will respond, and we will know his will.

CRUMBS

I think I heard the bell calling us to supper, Vinnie.

You sure did, boss. Let's go.

What do you mean, "let's?" I think that bell was intended for the priests.

I know that, boss, but nobody wants to eat alone, so I thought I would tag along just to keep you guys company.

That's very thoughtful of you, Vinnie. Are you sure that's the only reason you want to go to the table with us?

Ah, boss, you read me like a book. I must confess I had a faint hope that you might find it in your heart of hearts to toss a little parcel of food my way.

Now, Vinnie, how many times have I told you that eating from the table is not good for you? How are you ever going to lose weight by eating table scraps?

I know that, boss, but I'll just lie here by the table and watch you eat in case you experience a change of heart.

Be my guest, Vinnie, but don't think you're going to talk me into giving you something just by looking at me with those woeful eyes.

I wouldn't consider it, boss. I just enjoy watching you taking one big bite after another, while I sit here at your feet practically famished with hunger.

Nice try, Vinnie, but no cigar.

No problem, boss, but if you don't mind, I think I'll just mosey on out to the kitchen to see what Sister is doing.

Don't you mean you're going to try stealing something while Sister isn't looking?

Keep it down, boss, she may hear you.

Back already, Vinnie? You must not have had any luck out there.

I think Sister is on to me, boss. She keeps putting the stuff up where I can't reach it.

It may be that you've stolen just one too many sticks of butter, Vinnie.

That could be, boss, because it's getting harder to find anything out in the kitchen. I'll just lie down here by the table and wait until you're finished.

I have to say, Vinnie, that you are being very patient. You never give up, do you?

Give up? Heavens no, boss. I know you too well for that.

Oh, all right. Here's a little scrap of meat, but don't tell anybody. They'll yell at me.

Crumbs the word, boss. Thanks.

Reflection:

1. What signs are there to remind me of God's love for me?
2. Do I place my trust in God's love, even when I can't feel it?
3. Have there been times when God answered my prayer in a way I didn't expect?

TWENTY-FIRST SUNDAY IN ORDINARY TIME

Matthew 16:13-20

Our journey through life is something like a treasure hunt. We are always on the hunt for something that will satisfy all our wants and needs, and it always seems to be just bit too far away, or too elusive, slipping from our grasp just when we thought we had found it. This elusive treasure is what Jesus calls the Kingdom of Heaven. It is a place where all we are looking for is ours. The words and actions of Jesus teach us that he is the treasure we seek. To ensure that none of us are locked out of the Kingdom, he has entrusted his Church with the key to open the door to the Kingdom of Heaven. We need not fear we will be excluded. We need only to follow the guidance offered in our Church.

KEY MOMENTS

What's the problem, boss? Why are we slowing down?

I'm looking for something, Vinnie. I can't seem to find my key.

Which key is that, boss?

The key to our house.

The key to our house?! What do you mean you can't find the key? All my food is in the house.

Now just calm down, Vinnie. I'm sure I have it here somewhere. Don't worry, you're not going to starve.

All right, all right, boss, but let's think about this for a moment. What if you can't find the key? Then what are we going to do?

That's a good question, Vinnie. Do you have any ideas?

We're going to have to find another way to get into the house, aren't we boss? Maybe I could put my 'bury the bone' skills to work.

Just how do you intend to do that?

I could start digging. I'm pretty good at that.

You'll get no argument from me on that, Vinnie, but I'm afraid we would have a long wait before we got into the house that way.

Why do you say that, boss? I can bury a bone in two seconds flat.

Yes, Vinnie, but our house has a deep foundation, and you would have to dig down about ten feet.

You have a point there, boss. I'm not sure I want to go to all that trouble. Let's think of something else.

We could try climbing in a window. You might have trouble getting up that high, but I could give you a lift.

That's a possibility, boss, but what if all the windows are locked?

That's a problem, Vinnie. I suppose we could break a window, but I really don't want to do that.

Bad idea, boss. Think of something else.

I'm trying to, Vinnie, but it's not easy to get into a locked house without a key.

It's not supposed to be, boss, that's why it's a good idea to make sure you have a key when you leave the house, but let's not go there now. Are you sure you don't have the key? Did you check all your pockets?

I did, Vinnie, but I'm not worried, because I have the answer to our problem. We'll just borrow a phone and call someone and ask them to open the house for us.

Of course! Why didn't I think of that, boss? It's a good thing you let someone else have the key to our house.

Reflection:

1. Am I keeping abreast of the directions the Church is going by engaging in ongoing instruction and reading?
2. What are my feelings toward the Church I belong to?
3. What can I do to make my Church more attractive to those who are still seeking?

TWENTY-SECOND SUNDAY
IN ORDINARY TIME

Matthew 16:21-27

Some crosses are laid on our shoulders because life can be filled with unpleasant events. When that happens, we pray for the gift of patience to bear our cross and not lose faith. Such crosses are unavoidable and must be borne by everyone. Other crosses are the ones we take upon ourselves. They come as a result of choices we make to follow in the footsteps of Jesus, who says we must be willing to "take up our cross" to be his follower. When one makes a conscious decision to be a disciple, it must follow that one chooses to accept the crosses that come as a result of that decision. The ways of the world will always be a temptation for us to abandon the cross of discipleship. There is no place for the cross in the philosophy of the world. As Christians, we believe that sometimes the only way to relieve pain is to accept it as a blessing and a call from the Lord.

A SMALL PRICE TO PAY

It sure is a nice day today, boss. What do we have lined up for today?

This is a special day for you, Vinnie. You've been invited to be the guest of honor at a pet blessing.

That's right. I remember you telling me about that some time ago. Well, that's great, I'll just lounge around until we have to leave.

It's not that easy, Vinnie. You can't go looking the way you do.

What's wrong with the way I look, boss? I look the same today as I did yesterday.

Yes, you do, Vinnie, but that's not what I mean. If we're going out as invited guests, then we need to get cleaned up.

Are you saying what I think I hear you saying, boss?

Now Vinnie, it's been a long time since you've had a bath, and it isn't going to hurt you that much.

It hasn't been long enough as far as I'm concerned, but I know there's no getting around it, boss, so let's get going and get it over with.

I knew you would understand, Vinnie, and to perfectly honest about it, you are better about taking a bath than many other dogs.

I don't know about that, boss, but I go along with the program because I know that's the price I have to pay as a church dog.

What makes you say that, Vinnie? How does being a church dog have anything to do with it?

It's pretty obvious, boss. Think of all the people whom I have to greet each day. You know they're not content to just say hello, they have to run their fingers through my hair and let me know how happy they are to see me. I can't expect them to do all that if I'm not clean and shiny.

Good thinking, Vinnie, and besides that, you look so much better after you've had a bath. I'm sure people would rather see you looking good than all ragged and dirty.

I suppose so, boss. And now that I've achieved some fame as an author, it's even more incumbent that I look the part.

What's the "incumbent" stuff? You may be an author, Vinnie, but you don't have to start talking like one.

Sorry about that, boss. Sometimes I get carried away, so just carry me away and let's get this bath behind us.

Reflection:
1. What is the cross I being asked to carry right now?
2. Does this cross flow from my decision to be a disciple or is it just something that happens?
3. What can I do to make this cross easier to carry?

TWENTY-THIRD SUNDAY IN ORDINARY TIME

Matthew 18:15-20

The Scriptures are clear in teaching that no one travels the road to heaven alone. God chose a people, not an individual. We are a community of faith and our faith finds expression in our relationships to one another. Some prefer to walk the journey alone, thinking that church membership and participation is an option. While such a choice may eliminate some of the problems we encounter in our dealings with one another, it is not the way Jesus prescribes. We must learn to work out our differences as a community. Jesus blesses this effort by promising to be present when we gather in his name.

LET'S GET TOGETHER

I'm home, Vinnie. Did you have a nice day while I was away?

It was all right, boss, but I prefer it when you stay home.

I know that, but I hope you didn't get too depressed.

Oh no, boss. There were plenty of people here for me to hang out with, and there are always those who come to visit while you're away. I like to greet them and let them know they are welcome.

That's great, Vinnie, and I'm sure they are glad to see you.

That goes without saying, boss. There's nothing like a friendly greeting from the church dog to warm people's hearts.

Well, I'm home now, so perhaps we can get back to normal. If you don't mind, I'm going upstairs for a while to do some reading.

That's perfectly all right, boss. You go ahead. I'll wait for you.

I'm finished reading, Vinnie, I'll be right down.

No need to shout, boss, I'm right here.

Oh, excuse me. I thought you were still downstairs. What are you doing up here? You never come upstairs.

I was wandering around down there, but I couldn't find anyone, so I came upstairs.

I guess you're right, Vinnie. I think all the priests are in their own rooms.

I figured that out for myself, boss, so I came up here.

You could have waited downstairs. You know we would all be coming down there eventually.

I suppose so, boss. But I didn't feel like waiting. I like to be where the action is, and right now all the action is upstairs, even if all of you are very quiet up here.

Well, I'm heading for the living room now. You're welcome to join me there.

Thanks, boss, but I think I'll just wait awhile until the other guys are ready to come down.

All right, I'll see you in a little bit.

Did Vinnie come down with any of you? I haven't seen him.

He was lying in the hallway when I came down. Here he comes now.

Hi guys. If you don't mind I'll just lie down here. It's nice to be with all of you again. It doesn't get any better.

Reflection:

1. How do we respond to those who think going to church is unnecessary?
2. How much are we involved in our own church community?
3. Does praying together bring a sense of peace to me?

TWENTY-FOURTH SUNDAY IN ORDINARY TIME

Matthew 18:21-35

There is probably no other command of Jesus as difficult for us as the command to forgive. It appears several times in the gospels and, especially, in the prayers Jesus taught us: "forgive us our trespasses as we forgive one another." Forgiving those who hurt us may take time, but in the time it takes, we do well to remember the many times we have been forgiven by God. How many personal and even world problems could be resolved if only we could learn to forgive one another?

ALL IS FORGIVEN

Did you enjoy your visit with George today, Vinnie?

George who?

The little dog that came to visit you today.

Oh, that George. Yes, we had a very nice time.

What did the two of you do?

I took him over to my toy box so he could pick out a toy to play with and then we ran around the house to see if there was anyone who wanted to play catch with us.

Did you have any success?

Not much. Everybody was too busy to play.

I'm sorry to hear that. What did you do then?

Since the toy caper didn't work, I found someone to open the door so we could go outside. George enjoyed sniffing around the yard. Those were some smells he hadn't smelled before, so he enjoyed doing that.

And what did you do while that was going on?

I just lay there and watched. I knew all those smells, so it wasn't necessary for me to go with him.

It sounds like you two got along pretty well together.

Yes, we did, boss. Sometimes it's nice to have another dog like myself to play with.

I hope there was enough water for both of you to drink.

There was plenty of water, boss. However, I did encounter one little problem.

And what was that?

You see, after George left, I went to eat my food, but there wasn't any.

What do you think happened, Vinnie?

I know what happened. George must have been hungry when he arrived this morning, so he went and helped himself to my food.

I didn't know that. Do you mean to say that even though he ate all your food, you played with him as though nothing had happened?

Sure, boss. I was a little peeved at first, but I forgave him after that.

I'm a little surprised at that, Vinnie, knowing how much you look forward to eating.

It wasn't easy, boss, but then I thought of all the times you fed me and how you don't get mad when I steal your food, and then it was easy to forgive George.

Reflection:
1. Think of all the blessings God has bestowed upon you.
2. How many times have you needed to ask for God's forgiveness?
3. Is there anyone still waiting for your forgiveness?

TWENTY-FIFTH SUNDAY IN ORDINARY TIME

Matthew 20:1-16a

Among those who work to earn a living, there is always the temptation to think that those who are living on assistance are unworthy of the help they receive. We tend to criticize them as lazy and shiftless, thinking they ought to work for a living like the rest of us. Undoubtedly that may be true for some people, but the generosity of God toward those who worked shorter hours is an invitation to all of us to reconsider. In many instances, those who do not work cannot work. Perhaps there are simply no jobs or the jobs that are available would require losing health benefits. Perhaps there are family duties or physical disabilities. The workers who came late may not have been able to come earlier, or because of limited talents were the last to be hired. Whatever the reason, and even for no reason, God sees fit to reward them like all the others.

WHAT A GUY!

It's almost suppertime, boss, shouldn't we be heading to the table?

You're right, Vinnie. Let's go and see what's for supper.

I'm really hungry, boss. I hope there's something there for me.

What makes you so hungry, Vinnie? Did you work hard today?

Well now, let's see, boss. Besides taking you for your walk, there were a few other duties I had to attend to.

And what were those, Vinnie? I can't say I saw you working too hard.

They may not seem hard to you, boss, but they were taxing.

Tell me about it, Vinnie.

For starters, I had several calls to answer at the door. That involves a lot of running around, you know.

Maybe so, Vinnie, but it doesn't appear all that difficult to me, and I've noticed that once you've greeted our visitors you don't hang around very long.

I am getting a little older, boss, and I need to get my rest.

Yes, of course. And what else did you do that was so exhausting?

I helped Eileen in the office. She had a lot of work to do, so I stayed with her to help her out.

Now hold on just a minute, Vinnie. Whenever I pass Eileen's office, you're either lying on the floor resting or standing at her desk begging. That doesn't look like a whole lot of work to me.

I'll admit, it's not the hardest thing I have to do, but somebody's got to do it, and I'm the guy.

I suppose you're going to tell me you also helped Karen with the cleaning?

Of course I did, boss. How else could she get it done?

And just what do you do to help?

Not a whole lot, but I'm there in case there's a bit of work that calls for a dog. You know, she may run into one of those critters that I can take of.

In other words, you just lie around and watch. And all of that exhausting activity is what makes you so hungry? To tell you the truth Vinnie, I don't think it's that impressive.

But boss, don't blame me. I am just a dog after all. I'm doing the best I can.

That's true, Vinnie. You did your best. Have a biscuit.

Thanks, boss. What a guy!

Reflection:
1. Do I look upon the work I do as a gift from God?
2. What is my attitude toward helping those who do not work?
3. Am I aware of the problems which sometimes make work impossible for others?

TWENTY-SIXTH SUNDAY
IN ORDINARY TIME

Matthew 21:28-32

God is always ready to forgive our past transgressions and allow us to start anew. God also holds us accountable for the present and we cannot presume that because we have done good things in the past that we need not worry about the present. In the gospel story of the two sons, one son is saved because of a change of heart which prompts him to do the right thing; the second son is condemned for not acting on the promise he has made. There is a third son, not mentioned in the gospel, but whose presence is implied. That third son would be the ideal son who both promises to do the father's will and also follows through on that promise. That is the ideal we must strive for.

MAKE UP YOUR MIND

It feels good to finally sit down and rest, Vinnie. This has been a long day, don't you agree? What's that, Vinnie? I didn't hear you say anything.

I'm waiting, boss.

What are you waiting for?

I'm waiting to go out.

Why didn't you say something before I sat down?

I wasn't sure I wanted to go out just then.

That was one minute ago!

Let's not get technical, boss, just open the door and let me out.

All right, all right, just be patient.

Hey, boss, I'm out here.

No kidding? I seem to remember just letting you out about two minutes ago.

It's not as interesting out here as I thought it was, so let me in.

All right, I'm coming.

Thanks, boss, I think I'll just lie here and rest a while.

I hope so, Vinnie.

Did you hear that, boss?

I didn't hear anything, Vinnie. I was just enjoying the quiet.

Your ears aren't what they used to be, boss. I'm sure I heard something out there.

I suppose you want to go out and investigate.

You're learning, boss, just open the door.

All right, but why don't you stay out there for a while just in case something else catches your ear?

I'll think about it, boss.

It's me, boss. I need to come in.

Already? You just went out.

I know, but I forgot something.

Now what?

Just a minute, boss, I'll be right back.

Is that what you forgot, your toy puppy?

Right, boss. It was a little lonely out there, so I needed some company.

Are you going to stay out now? Are you sure you have everything you need? I wouldn't want to inconvenience you in any way.

No problem, boss. I'll let you know if I'm missing anything. See you later.

Reflection:

1. Is there something in my life that needs turning around?
2. Am I confident that God will forgive me for past mistakes?
3. Do I accept God's will without grumbling and complaint?

TWENTY-SEVENTH SUNDAY IN ORDINARY TIME

Matthew 21:33-43

So many times we wait for the Lord to enter our lives and answer our prayers. Sometimes the Lord does come into our lives and provides the answers we need, but we fail to recognize his presence, because the answers we receive are not the answers we are looking for. For years God's people awaited the coming of the Messiah. God did send them the Messiah, but Jesus was not the Messiah they expected, so that when he came, they refused to accept him. We must always be prepared to accept the presence of the Lord in our lives, even when his appearance does not meet our expectations.

JUST WHAT YOU WANTED

Is that you, boss?

Yes, Vinnie, I'm home.

Did you have a nice day off?

It was beautiful, Vinnie. This time of the year is probably the nicest of all.

Yes, yes, boss, but let's not waste time. What did you bring me?

Was I supposed to bring you something?

Don't get cute, boss. You know you always bring me something when you come home from your day off.

Is that why you're so happy to see me?

That's part of it, boss. So, what did you buy for me?

Well, I didn't forget about you, Vinnie. As a matter of fact I did a lot of shopping and I have several treats for you to choose from.

Bully for you, boss. Let's see what they are.

First, I have this thing that looks like a bone and is filled with something that is supposed to taste like peanut butter. See how you like it.

Let me give it a smell, boss.

Well, what do you think?

What else do you have?

There's this nice piece of rawhide which looks like it's been basted in some kind of meat gravy. I thought you might like to try it.

That looks pretty good, boss, but I have found that these things look better than they taste. I don't know what they do to them, but whatever it is, I'm not impressed.

I take it that means you're not interested in this one.

You might conclude that, boss, but let's not rule anything out just yet.

Maybe this last one will catch your fancy. What in heavens name is that thing, boss?

I'm not sure, Vinnie, but it looks a little like an extra thick piece of bacon.

Now if really were an extra thick piece of bacon, that would be great, but you know as well as I, boss, that it isn't.

No, of course it isn't, but it does smell a bit like bacon, doesn't it?

Yes, a bit, but a bit of bacon smell can't fool me. That's some kind of healthy stuff made to look and smell like something I might like.

All of these are good for you, Vinnie, but you've got to choose one and enjoy it.

Just leave them, boss. Maybe I'll try one later.

Reflection:
1. What are the needs for which I am praying to God?
2. What exactly do I want God to do for me?
3. Has God ever answered my prayers in ways I didn't expect?

TWENTY-EIGHTH SUNDAY IN ORDINARY TIME

Matthew 22-1-14

There is nothing more embarrassing than showing up for a celebration wearing the wrong clothes. Sometimes we are overdressed; other times we are underdressed. Either way, we feel very uncomfortable and would like to run home and change clothes. Experience teaches us it is not enough to simple show up in response to an invitation. We have to show up wearing the proper clothes. It is no less true of our invitation to the heavenly wedding feast. Simply being baptized and confirmed is not enough. These are the invitations we receive to enter more deeply into the life of Christ, but we must respond to the invitations constantly throughout our lives by living the Christ-life we have received.

ALL DRESSED UP

What's that you're reading, boss?

I'm just looking over my mail, and there's something here you may be interested in, Vinnie.

What's that, boss?

It's an invitation for you to speak.

Another one of those, boss? You know it's hard for me to get up and speak in front of others. I get very nervous.

But wait, Vinnie, this one's a little different from the others.

What's so different about this one?

This one is from young people at a school pretty far away. It means you and I are going to have to travel.

Oh man, boss, this is getting harder and harder. I'm not a great fan of riding in the car, although it can be interesting at times.

Well what can I do to make it interesting for you, Vinnie? Maybe it won't be as bad as you think.

Let me put it to you this way, boss. Are there any horses or cows along the way that I can speak to?

Do you call that speaking, Vinnie? I always thought you were just barking your fool head off.

Listen, boss, those animals are a bit dense, and you have to speak up in order to be heard.

If you say so, Vinnie, but what do you think— should we accept this invitation or not?

That's the question, isn't it, boss? Let's think about it a minute.

All right, you have one minute, so tell me what you think.

Here's the thing, boss. We have been invited and obviously those young people would love to meet me.

Try to keep your head from getting too large, Vinnie. Let's just say they might enjoy meeting you.

Right, boss, and we should accept their invitation. It's the polite thing to do. So, what the heck, let's go.

All right, Vinnie, I agree, so now you had better get ready for your bath.

BATH? You didn't say anything about getting a bath.

But, Vinnie, you can't go visiting the way you look. You haven't had a bath in weeks and you want to look your best.

You're right, boss. Yes, of course, this is going to be a lot of fun and I want to be dressed for the occasion. I'll knock 'em out.

Reflection:

1. How does God invite me to enter more deeply into the life I have received?
2. What am I doing to nourish that life?
3. Is there some way I can respond even more completely to the invitation I have received?

TWENTY-NINTH SUNDAY IN ORDINARY TIME

Matthew 22:15-21

Jesus says we should give to Caesar what is Caesar's and to God what is God's. Most of us are good citizens and we keep the laws and pay our taxes, understanding that this is our duty to society. But giving to God what is God's— how do we measure that? All things are from God and there is no end to the debt we owe God. Perhaps it would be helpful to recognize that all we do, including our being good citizens, is a way of returning to God what is God's. It's all a matter of having the proper attitude in fulfilling the duties we have. We do them not because we want to avoid getting into trouble, but because this is God's will. Keeping the law and paying our taxes is yet another way of showing our love for God.

BLING

: flashy jewelry worn especially as an indication of wealth

Look here, Vinnie, this author says he took the collar off of his dog, because he didn't think the dog wanted all those medals and things jingling constantly. I never thought of that. Does that bother you?

To tell you the truth, boss, I don't give it much thought. I always thought you put it there to make me look better—like bling.

No, no, Vinnie that's not the case at all. Each one of your medallions has a practical purpose. You're already beautiful enough without me adding anything, besides which, I'm not a big fan of ostentatious jewelry.

You won't get an argument from me about that, boss, jewelry's not my bag. So what are all these things I'm wearing?

Let's take a look and see, Vinnie. This one was a gift to you. It is a St. Francis medal and it says: "St. Francis, protect my pet."

That's nice, boss. Let's keep that one, I can use some help from above.

You sure can, Vinnie. We all need help from above.

Let's see, now. This one lets us know that you've received your rabies vaccination.

Do I need that one, boss? I've never had rabies.

No you haven't, Vinnie, and that's because you've been vaccinated. That medal's a keeper.

Any more, boss?

Yes, this gold one in the shape of a dog biscuit has all the information you'll need in case you get lost. It tells the person who finds you who you are and where you live.

That sounds like a good idea, boss. There's not much chance I would ever be lost, but we'll hold to that one just in case.

And finally, Vinnie, there's this dog tag that says "Ohio Dog."

Now wait a minute, boss. I think it's perfectly obvious that I'm an Ohio dog without a tag to tell me about it.

But Vinnie, this is something you have to wear. It's the law.

Sounds like a silly law to me, boss, but if there's no other way, I'll wear it if it'll make you happy.

That's the best reason of all, Vinnie.

Reflection:

1. What is my attitude toward paying taxes?
2. In what way do my taxes help others?
3. What am I doing to show my appreciation for God's gifts?

THIRTIETH SUNDAY
IN ORDINARY TIME

Matthew 22-34—40

Jesus says we must love God with all our heart, soul and mind. This is the first commandment, and the second is like it: love your neighbor as yourself. The key word in understanding what Jesus was saying is the word "like." "Like" can mean "similar", so that the two commandments are similar to each other, in that they both deal with love. This explanation seems weak and incomplete. "Like" could also mean "identical", so that there is no difference between the two. This is closer to the spirit of the text, but fails to distinguish between the two. Perhaps Jesus wants to tell us that loving our neighbor is but another way of loving God, different from loving God, but at the same time an act of love for God.

TRUE LOVE

Vinnie, look at all these toys scattered around the house. Is it really necessary for you to have so many toys? Look at your toy box. It's overflowing with your stuffed animals and things.

But, boss, those are the tools of my trade. I need all those different stuffed animals for my job.

What job is that, Vinnie?

You know, taking care of all the people who come to visit us.

Is it really necessary to bring all of them a toy?

I don't suppose it is, boss, but I think they appreciate that I am thinking of them.

That's very considerate of you, Vinnie, and you don't even know most of the people you come to greet.

No, I don't, boss, but that doesn't mean I shouldn't care about them. I guess it comes under the rubric of loving your neighbor.

There's no question about that, Vinnie. Do you treat everybody the way you treat the people who come to the door?

I wouldn't say that, boss. For example, you and I meet a lot of people when we are out walking, but if you notice, I don't pay much attention to them.

I have noticed that, Vinnie, and that's probably a good thing. If we had to stop and greet everybody we see, we might never finish our walk.

That's right, boss, that's the way I see it. We've got to just keep on walking, although you'll notice I do stop when somebody wants to pet me. I figure that's the right and proper thing to do.

Absolutely, Vinnie, those people might need a little extra love.

You'll also notice, boss, that for the most part I don't pay much attention to people driving by us in their cars.

Not unless they have a dog in the car, Vinnie, and in those cases you're almost out of control. I think you'd run right after those cars if I didn't have a leash on you.

True, boss, but there it's not the people I'm greeting, it's my fellow dogs. We have to stick together, you know.

So tell me, Vinnie, why is it that you are so nice to the people who come to our house?

It's this way, boss, those people are your friends and when I entertain them; I'm really doing it for you. Think of it, boss. How could I say I'm helping you, if I don't help your friends?

Reflection:
1. In what ways have I loved my neighbor today?
2. When I make an effort to help others, do I ever think of it as an act of love for God?
3. Be prepared to respond to an opportunity to show love to your neighbor.

My goodness, that poor dog is so clean and brushed
that a squirel would walk right under it's nose and never
even know it was a dog.

BRIDGET NEUGEBAUER

THIRTY-FIRST SUNDAY
IN ORDINARY TIME

Matthew 23:1-12

Jesus had little use for those who reduced religion to obtaining status and titles, while neglecting the practice of true religion. There is a place for recognizing the position and attending responsibilities of those who hold high positions in the church, the purpose of these positions should serve only to enable the church to be more effective in its ministry to others. Regardless of our place in the order of things, we are all able to carry out the wishes of Our Lord to serve one another.

PUTTING ON AIRS

What are you watching, Vinnie?

Nothing important, boss. It's just this dog show on television.

I should think you would find that interesting, Vinnie, after all those are some prize dogs you're looking at.

I suppose they are, boss, but to tell you the truth, I'm not impressed.

Don't tell me you're jealous, Vinnie.

Heck no, boss. You wouldn't catch me dead appearing in one of those shows. As a matter of fact, I feel sorry for those poor dogs.

That's an interesting observation, Vinnie. Why do you say that?

Because they've got those dogs all spruced up to the point they don't even look like real dogs anymore. Now look at that one, boss. My goodness, that poor dog is so clean and brushed that a squirrel would walk right under its nose and never even know it was a dog.

But that's the way that dog's boss wants the dog to look, Vinnie. That dog is groomed in order to impress the judges.

That's the whole point, boss. Look at the judges.

They look like nice people to me, Vinnie.

I'm sure they are, boss, but that's my point: they're people. Do you see any dogs among those judges?

Of course not, Vinnie

But what do people know about what makes one dog better than another? Only dogs know that, boss.

So you're saying that dressing a dog up to look beautiful doesn't mean that the well dressed dog is better than other dogs?

All you can say, boss, is that it's better looking, but looks mean nothing to us dogs, boss. We judge a dog by how well it does what it is supposed to do.

Giving a dog a bath and hair-do doesn't make it a better hunter or shepherd.

I think I see your point, Vinnie. Those dogs may look the way people want them to look, but sometimes people don't appreciate what makes a dog a really good dog.

Now you're beginning to understand it, boss. That's why I feel sorry for those dogs. My guess is that they really are good dogs, but all this fussing over them is depriving them from being what they really are—dogs. They would be much happier if they could just serve their boss the way they're supposed to do. That's what makes me happy boss, just being good old, at your service, Vinnie.

Reflection:
1. Who am I called to serve?
2. How am I serving them?
3. Are there others I might be able to serve?

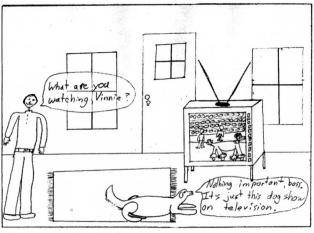

What are you watching, Vinnie?
Nothing important, boss. It's just this dog show on television.   JOE WELLEMEYER

THIRTY THIRD SUNDAY
IN ORDINARY TIME

Matthew 25:14-30

God has given each of us gifts to be used for our own happiness and to be used to make this world a better place. We must never question the gifts we have by failing to recognize them or by comparing them to the gifts others have. The person we are is the person we are meant to be and the person God wants us to be. The reminder that some day the Master will return to demand an accounting of us should also serve to call to mind that our time on this earth is limited and we must take advantage of the time allotted to us. Every day is a blessing and an opportunity to put our gifts and talents to work.

PAINFUL LESSONS

Is that you out there, boss?

Yes, it is, Vinnie, I've come to take you home.

I won't give you an argument about that, boss, this has been quite an ordeal, and I'm glad it's over.

While we're waiting for the doctor to sign you out, why don't you tell me about it, Vinnie?

I'd love to, boss. It all started on Sunday evening, when I wasn't feeling well.

Yes, I noticed that, Vinnie, that's when I took you to see your doctor.

Right, boss, I remember that. And the next thing I know I'm out here in this hospital and they start taking all kinds of pictures. I don't know why they had to do that, I have plenty of pictures of myself.

Yes, Vinnie, but these pictures showed what was going on inside of you, and it wasn't good. You had something very large growing inside of you.

Holy cow, boss! I didn't know that. What was it?

That's what we had to find out, Vinnie, so you needed some surgery.

So that's where this cut on my belly came from. Well, what did they find, boss? Nothing serious, I hope.

Not what I was afraid of, but serious nevertheless. It seems one of your kidneys was not functioning and was causing you a lot of problems, so they took out your kidney and your spleen.

Is that all right, boss? I mean, can I live without those things?

Sure, Vinnie, you just need some time to heal, and you'll be back to your old self.

I'm glad to hear that, boss. You had me worried there for a while.

Not as worried as you had me, Vinnie. Let's just say, we're both glad it's over.

You know, boss, while I was in the hospital, I had some time to think.

What did you think about, Vinnie?

I thought of how short life can be and how grateful I am for it. I also realized I need to use well the time I have, because time is so precious. I think I'll be a better church dog than ever.

Good boy, Vinnie. Maybe your stay here did more good than we thought.

Right boss, but now, let's you and me go home.

Reflection:
1. What gifts has God given me?
2. Am I sometimes jealous of the gifts of others?
3. What am I doing to make good use of my time?

THIRTY-FOURTH OR LAST SUNDAY IN ORDINARY TIME

Matthew 25:31-46

CALLED TO HIGHER THINGS

St. John of the Cross says that in the evening of life we will be judged on love. The gospel account of the final judgment specifies that this love should be directed especially to those in need of any kind. God has planted the seeds of that love in our hearts, leading us to sympathize with the plight of the poor and suffering. Putting that sympathy into practice is the way we can bring the love of God from heaven to earth. At the end of our life, the love we have shown on earth will lead us to the joys of heaven.

How are you feeling today, Vinnie? It's been a while now since your surgery, so you should be getting back to normal.

I think I'm getting there, boss, but it's taking me longer than I thought.

I'm not surprised, Vinnie, after all, you're not as young as you used to be.

You're right about that, boss, but I wish I would get better so I could go out with you for our afternoon walks.

That will come, Vinnie, you just have to be patient.

I'm trying, boss, and in the meantime I've been doing a lot of thinking.

What have you been thinking about?

I've been thinking about how nice everybody has been to me, asking about me and feeding me real people food. It seems now that I'm sick, people care about me more than ever.

That's how people are, Vinnie. We pay special attention to those who are in any kind of need. I guess we just feel sorry for them.

I've noticed that, boss. I don't think dogs are like that. I remember my own parents. They did what they had to do, and then they just left us pups to fend for ourselves, and as you know, I didn't fend so well. Not until I arrived here.

Maybe that's one of the big differences between dogs and humans, Vinnie. I guess you just don't have that planted in you the way we do, but you know what, Vinnie, sometimes we need a little reminder too.

What kind of reminder are you speaking of, boss?

Well, God made us to be like himself, but sometimes we forget and don't take care of people the way we should.

I get it, boss, you need to be reminded to be the kind of person you are called to be. You're supposed to be like God and take care of all the people, like myself, who need special attention.

That's right, Vinnie.

That's really something, boss. Just think, by taking care of me the way you do, you're acting just like God.

That's right, Vinnie.

Do you think I could learn to act the way you do and become almost human?

That's an interesting question, Vinnie. Why not?

Golly boss, maybe all that people food is good for me. I think we should consider keeping me on this diet.

Reflection:

1. Who are the needy I am called to serve and assist?
2. How am I responding to those in need?
3. Is there more I could do?

SOLEMNITIES DURING ORDINARY TIME

THE SOLEMNITY OF
THE MOST HOLY TRINITY
John 3:16-18

One of the most important words in today's gospel is the word "gave". When God gave us Jesus, the gift had no strings attached. God literally gave over to us the gift of his son. The gift God gave was total and complete. There was no holding back. So generous was God's gift that God did not stop until the very life of his Son had been taken. God gave his son as a gift, not a loan. God's love is an example for all of us who are called to walk in the footsteps of Jesus. Each of us is called in some way to lay down our lives for others—to give without counting the cost. When a person pledges their love for another, as in marriage, that love will demand the total giving of self. Unless the gift is complete, the marriage will not be complete. Such commitments must be thought through and entered with eyes open.

ALL OR NOTHING

Wake up, boss!

I am awake. Can't you see that I'm busy?

You don't look very busy to me. You're just sitting there doing nothing.

I'm not doing "nothing." I'm reading the newspaper; at least I was reading the newspaper. So, what is it you want, Vinnie?

I brought you my stuffed puppy toy.

Thank you very much.

Well, what are you going to do with it, boss?

I'll just keep here with me.

That's not what you're supposed to do, boss!

What am I supposed to do?

You're supposed to throw it, so I can run after it.

I knew there was a catch to this so-called gift.

Okay, boss. I'm ready. Let 'er fly.

Are you back already, Vinnie? I thought I might get a moment's rest.

I may be getting older, boss, but I've still got some of that old zip left in me. Here, try again.

All right, here goes, Vinnie, keep your eyes peeled.

That was a good one, boss. Your aim is improving.

Thanks, Vinnie. C'mon, let's try it again. Let go.

Not this time, boss. I think I'll hold on to it for a while.

Now just a minute, Vinnie, you told me you had brought me this present, and now you're taking it back again? What kind of present is that?

I changed my mind, boss. I decided to keep it for myself.

But Vinnie, when you give someone a gift, you're not supposed to take it back again. That's not a real gift.

If you'll remember, boss, I never told you it was a gift. I just said I brought it to you, so you could throw it and I could retrieve it. That's what we retrievers do.

I think you're missing something, Vinnie. Retrievers are supposed to retrieve and bring the duck, rabbit or whatever back and give it to their masters.

That's what I did, boss.

Yes, but the whole idea is to give the master the object of his hunt. You're not supposed to hold on to it.

Do you mean, when I give you a gift I have to let go of it completely?

That's right, Vinnie. That's what giving means.

Nobody ever told me that, boss. I'm not sure I want to go that far. Let me think about it and I'll get back to you.

Reflection:

1. In what ways do I find it difficult to give totally of myself?
2. Who are the people in my life that deserve the most of me?
3. How much do I give of myself to those not especially close to me?

THE SOLEMNITY OF
THE MOST HOLY BODY
AND BLOOD OF CHRIST

John 6:51-58

For many of us, taking the time to provide spiritual nourishment for our souls is difficult. It is always easier to postpone our efforts to pray or go to church, because the food this world offers seems more interesting and attractive. Our time is so limited and there is so much to do in the space of 24 hours, that often there is little time left for spiritual matters. Taking time for prayer and spiritual reading requires a commitment which leads us to build time into our daily schedule and then adhere to it. Unless we mark out the time we need, we find that there is no room left in our busy lives for these important moments. Perhaps it is a question of determining what is most important and arranging our daily schedules based on our priorities.

IMPORTANT FOOD

You're eating your breakfast pretty early this morning, Vinnie.

Yes, boss, I haven't had anything since yesterday morning and I'm starved.

I'm glad you have such a healthy appetite, Vinnie, you must be in good health.

I think I am, boss. This food you give me seems to be doing the job, even though you can be a little stingy with it.

That's why you're so healthy, Vinnie. If I were any less stingy, you might be as wide as you are long.

Very funny, boss. Now if you don't mind, I would like to eat my meal in peace.

No problem, Vinnie. I'll see you later.

Hasta la vista, boss.

Yoo-hoo, Vinnie.

Did you call me, boss?

Yes, I thought you were eating early today because you were hungry.

I was, boss.

But you didn't eat everything. Look, you left all your big pieces on the bottom of your dish.

I know, boss, I was so filled up with the other food, that I didn't have room for those.

I can understand that, Vinnie, but do you know those pieces of food are the most important ones of all?

I can't say that I did, boss. Why do you say that?

Because those are there to help you remain as healthy and beautiful as you are.

Is that so? And just what do those little things do?

You see those three that all look alike. Those are specially made to promote a healthy coat and skin. Taking those three pills each morning keeps you from itching and shedding so much, and they give your coat that nice shine which makes you so attractive to the ladies.

Wow! Why didn't you tell me that earlier? Move over.

Good work, Vinnie, but there's still one pill left.

I'm a bit full. What's that one for?

That's to help you stay young and healthy. That's your senior vitamin pill.

Now hold on just one minute, boss. You're older than me. Do you take one of those things?

I do, Vinnie. You and I are both getting older and we need all the help we can get.

It's all gone, boss. I think I'll get a little rest now.

Reflection:

1. What are the things which keep me from spending time with God?
2. Have I built a time for God into my daily schedule?
3. Is prayer a priority for me?

SOLEMNITY OF
SAINT PETER AND SAINT PAUL

When Jesus left this earth, he promised not to leave us orphans. To fulfill that promise, not only did he send us the Holy Spirit, but he also placed Peter in charge as the head of the Church. Later he called Paul to take the gospel to the far corners of the world. These two apostles laid the foundations for the church, which would carry on the work of Jesus in his absence. Each of us is called in our own limited way to do whatever we can to promote the gospel of Jesus. We may be limited in our abilities, but we do whatever we can, trusting that the Lord will make up for our deficiencies.

IN CHARGE

I have to go away for a while, Vinnie, so you're on duty until I return.

What do you mean I'm "on duty?"

That means you're in charge of the house. Whatever happens, you take care of it.

Now hold there a minute, boss. How am I supposed to take care of things, when most of the things that happen around here, I can't do?

What are you referring to, Vinnie?

Well, for example, I can't answer the phone, and even if I could, I don't think the person on the other end would appreciate being barked at.

That's not a problem, Vinnie, our phones are set up to answer themselves so people don't need to get barked at, they can just leave a message.

All right, boss, I can live with that, but to tell you the truth, they would probably prefer to get barked at.

So you see, Vinnie. It won't be a problem for you to take charge.

There is one other situation that may be difficult for me to handle, boss.

What's that, Vinnie?

The door. What am I supposed to do if the children come to the door for cookies? I don't know how to open the door.

Now that is a problem, Vinnie. It's not so much that you couldn't open the door. The problem would be in your getting the cookies to the door.

Hey, come on, boss. I would be happy to share the cookies with the children.

Who said anything about sharing, Vinnie? You're supposed to give the cookies to the children, not share the cookies with them.

If I can't answer the phone or open the door, just what am I supposed to do while you're away?

234

Just do what you do best, guard the house and don't let anybody in.

That's all, boss? That's a piece of cake.

That's all there is to it, Vinnie. If anything else happens, I'll take care of it when I get back.

I guess I can handle it, boss. It won't be done the same as if you were here, but I'll get the job done and the place won't fall apart while you're gone.

That's the spirit, Vinnie. I knew I could count on you.

No problem, boss. I'll take charge while you're gone, but do hurry back, I'll miss you.

REFLECTION:

1. What were the gifts and shortcomings of St. Peter and St. Paul?
2. Why did Jesus choose these two men?
3. How can I best use my talents to promote the work of the church?

THE ASSUMPTION OF THE BLESSED VIRGIN MARY

Luke 1:39-56

Mary's "Magnificat" identifies her as one of God's little ones—the people of the land who are poor and unnoticed, the people for whom God has a special love. Knowing of God's goodness, these poor people depend completely on God to supply the things they need. Mary's greatness comes from the call she has received from God to be the mother of his son. There is much we can do with the talents God has given to us, but all our gifts will be even more valuable when we use them to respond to God's call, knowing that all we are and can become comes to us from God.

MORE THAN YOU CAN BE

There's somebody at the door, boss. I don't know who it is, but I think they want to come in.

Hold on a second, Vinnie, I'll be right there.

I'll wait here to greet them, boss.

Well, what do you know, Vinnie, these people have come all the way from Cleveland to see you.

No kidding? Why do they want to see me?

Because you're so well known. They have been reading about you, and they want to meet you.

Golly, I didn't think I was that important. There are a lot of other dogs just like me. That's really something, isn't it, boss?

What do you mean, Vinnie?

Just think about it, boss. It wasn't so long ago that I was just another puppy no one wanted. I was no different than any other dog. If anything, I was even less important than other dogs, and I could easily have been sent to the pound for you know what. And look at me now. People are travelling to see me and bring me things.

I never thought of it that way, Vinnie, because you've always been special to me, but now that you mention it, it's true.

Sometimes I have to pinch myself, boss, to make sure I'm not dreaming. There is so much here that I never imagined I would have. I've got a beautiful house to live in, all the food I need, and so many friends. What more could a dog ask for?

Not much, Vinnie. And now, in addition to all that, you have people coming to visit you from out of town. You're like a celebrity.

Right, boss, and I owe it all to you for taking me in and giving me a home.

Perhaps, Vinnie, but I think you could have done pretty well on your own. After all, you are a very nice dog.

I can't disagree with that, boss, but you have to realize there are limitations to what dog can do, even a dog as nice as me,. Dogs really depend on the people they live with to give them the extras that dogs on their own don't enjoy. Without people, dogs live a pretty ordinary life, looking for food and a place to stay each day.

You're right, Vinnie. You do have to depend on others, don't you?

Yes, and when you find the right person, boss, you can live like a king. And now, would you show in my visitors?

Reflection:
1. How has God blessed me in my life?
2. Do I regularly praise God for what He has done for me?
3. Am I using my gifts to serve God and others?

THE EXALTATION
OF THE HOLY CROSS

John 3:13-17

Today we decorate the cross and make it out of precious metals. Sometimes it is bedecked with jewels. Why go to such expense to form a piece of jewelry? Because we know that the cross is the means by which Jesus saved our souls, and in honoring the cross, we are honoring the One who gave his life upon that cross, so that each of us could be saved. The cross is a sign of the infinite, self-giving love God has for us. Wearing the cross and honoring it in our homes and churches is a reminder to us that, like Jesus, we are called to give our lives to one another in countless acts of self-sacrificing love.

PRICELESS

Vinnie, I need to ask you a question.

What's that, boss?

People keep asking me why you are always barking when you go outside.

That's easy, boss, it's my job.

It is? Why do you say that that?

Can't you see, boss, I'm not barking just for the fun of it. I'm barking at those people and things that might be a danger to you. It's my way of carrying out my duty to protect you guys.

I must admit, Vinnie, I never looked at it that way. I've never been aware of any danger in our courtyard. It seems pretty safe to me.

It may appear that way to you, boss, but that's why we dogs are needed. You can perceive danger only in the things you see; we sense it also with our noses. You might say we can smell it out.

If you say so, Vinnie, but it might be a good idea to tone it down a little. What do you say you and I go for our walk now? It seems like a pretty nice day.

Nice day or not, boss, I'm ready.

It must be a work day, boss, there's a lot of traffic out here.

There sure is, Vinnie, but no more than usual.

Whoops, hold on, boss, I see danger ahead.

What is it, Vinnie?

Can't you see it, boss? It's one of those trash pick up trucks. Here it comes—hold on.

Vinnie, take it easy, you're practically pulling my arm off! You can relax now, the truck is gone.

It had better be gone, boss, it's not a good idea to mess with me.

Really? And just what would you do if that truck decided not to listen to you and kept on going?

That's a good question, boss. I never thought about it.

Then let me tell you. You would not win that battle. If it comes down to you and that truck, you would lose. It may even cost you your life.

Ouch! Did you have to put it that way, boss?

I'm afraid it's the truth, Vinnie. That truck's a whole lot bigger than you are.

I suppose so, but that won't keep me from doing my job of protecting you, boss. That's the price I'll have to pay.

Thanks, Vinnie, that's what makes you so priceless.

Reflection:

1. Do I look upon the cross as more that a piece of jewelry?
2. What are the crosses the lord has laid upon my shoulders?
3. Have I accepted these crosses as a means of expressing my love for God and others?

Can't you see it, boss, it's one of those trash pick-up trucks. ALEX CAMPBELL

ALL SAINTS

Matthew 5:1-12a

From the earliest times, Christians honored those who gave their lives in defense of their faith, often placing their remains in the altars where Mass was celebrated. When the age of the martyrs, passed, men and women who displayed extraordinary virtue were recognized as saints, and honored as such by the church. We continue to look to those who lived saintly lives as models for ourselves, hoping to earn our crown of glory by walking in their footsteps. Not all saints are publicly recognized by the church, but we know that in our lives there have been those who inspired us to lead better lives, and we honor these each year on the feast of All Saints.

FOR ALL THE SAINTS

Look at that statue over there, Vinnie, there's dog at the feet of that saint.

Yes, of course, boss, that's a statue of St. Rock. He's the patron saint of dogs and dog lovers. We dogs have a special love for St. Rock.

That's a new one for me, Vinnie. How did St. Rock become so popular?

It goes like this, boss. Rock was born into a wealthy family, but he gave up all of that to go and serve the victims of the plague.

That sounds like a good thing to do, Vinnie. Rock must have been close to the Lord to be able to do that.

I think so, too, boss, but things didn't go all that well for Rock. It seems that sometimes the Lord forgets to take care of those who serve him.

Why do you say that, Vinnie?

Well, after working with all those sick people, Rock got sick himself.

You mean he came down with the plague.

Something like that, boss, but Rock was too kind to expect people to take care of him, so he went off by himself to die.

That was considerate of him, wasn't it Vinnie?

It sure was, boss, and that's why that dog you see in the statue came to his rescue.

You mean Rock didn't die after all?

No, boss, there was a dog that brought him food every day, until Rock was well enough to take care of himself.

I can see why Rock had a special love for his dog, Vinnie. That dog saved his life.

True, boss, and later when there was hardly any food for people to eat, Rock used to beg for just enough food for himself and his dog. I guess you could say Rock returned the favor.

That's a beautiful story, Vinnie. Where did you learn that?

It's all part of dog lore, boss. St. Rock's dog is right up there in our pantheon of dogs.

You mean there are other dogs as famous as St. Rock's dog?

O my yes, boss. You remember the dog that accompanied Tobias and Raphael on their journey home, and St. John Bosco's dog, that showed up to protect him at night. You see, boss, dogs are smart. They know they can become holy by hanging out with saints.

Reflection:
1. What do you know about your patron saint?
2. Do you have a favorite Saint?
3. Why do you choose this one?

THE DEDICATION OF THE LATERAN BASILICA IN ROME

John 2:13-22

With the shifting population of Catholics from one part of town to another, it is necessary to evaluate the need for parishes in the parts of town which no longer serve as they once did. This is a very painful process, and when a parish is forced to close its doors for a lack of people and needed financial resources, it is a tragedy for those who have lived there and whose memories are enshrined in those walls. There is no way to alleviate the pain for those who now must find a new church home, but it is good to remember that the Church is not a building, but a congregation of people, who are the living stones of the temple of God. Buildings must sometimes be left behind, but is never necessary to abandon the people who breathed life into the very walls of that building

A HOUSE IS NOT A HOME

Look over there, boss. Isn't that an awfully small house for people to live in?

It certainly is, Vinnie, but that house wasn't made for people. That's a dog house.

A dog house! For heaven's sake, why would any dog want to live in a house like that?

I should think it would be rather nice, Vinnie. Just think, you could have it decorated just the way you like, and you would have all the privacy you want.

That reminds me of my Uncle Rudy, boss.

Your uncle's name was Rudy? That a strange name for a dog.

His real name was Rodolphus D. Woofer, but we pups always called him Rudy.

So what is it about that dog house that makes you think of him?

It's a long story, boss, but I'll try to make it short for you. You see, Uncle Rudy had a dog house. I never quite knew what that meant until just now, but anyway, Uncle Rudy really seemed to like living by himself in that house, and I understand it was quite lavishly decorated with pictures of hamburgers and hot dogs on the walls, and a real bear skin rug to lie on.

It sounds like quite a house, Vinnie, so what happened?

Well, Uncle Rudy's boss and his family were moving out of the neighborhood, and they invited Uncle Rudy to go with them, but if he said yes, he would have to leave his dog house behind.

And what did Uncle Rudy do?

Be patient, boss, I'm coming to that.

Uncle Rudy decided he couldn't leave his wonderful house, so he opted to remain behind in his little castle when the boss and his family moved out.

Is that what he did?

Yes and no, boss. You see, once his family moved out, Uncle Rudy discovered that having his own house wasn't the same anymore. There was nobody to talk to and no children to play with.

So what did he do?

He packed up his things, left his house behind, and set out to find his family. He found them and he lived happily ever after. You see, boss, it isn't a house that makes a home; it's the people who live there.

Reflection:

1. Think of all that your parish means to you.
2. How would you feel if your parish had to close?
3. Would you be able to make the transition to another church building and another group of parishioners?

ST. VINCENT PARISH

St. Vincent Parish is located on the crest of Akron's West Hill, rising from the valley which once formed the basin for the Ohio canal. The history of St. Vincent is intimately connected to the history of the Ohio canal, which linked Lake Erie and the Ohio River.

In the early part of the nineteenth century, Irish immigrants began to arrive in America in great numbers. Their flight was precipitated by the Potato Famine, which claimed the lives of many in their native land. Willing to work wherever work was to be found, many of the Irish helped build the canal which brought industry and trade to Akron, Ohio.

In 1837, the pastor of St. Francis Xavier Church in nearby Doylestown began to visit these Irish Catholics, celebrating Mass in their homes, until a frame church was built in 1844. Construction on the present church began in 1864, and after a suspension of efforts during the Civil War, was completed in 1867.

Akron's first Catholic school began here in 1853. The parish still has an elementary school, while the high school has now merged and is known as St. Vincent-St. Mary High School.

St. Vincent continues to be an active parish serving the spiritual needs of its parishioners and providing education for its youth. The hard work and sacrifices of its first members continue to the present time, and St. Vincent is proud to be the first Catholic Church in Akron, Ohio.

CPSIA information can be obtained at www.ICGtesting.com
228237LV00001B/1/P

THROUGH THE YEAR WITH

VINNIE

CYCLE A

1999 — 2009

Rev. Joseph Kraker & Vinnie

Photos by David Shoenfelt
Illustrations by
Name of Children

PRESS